The Journals of Christian Daniel Claus and Conrad Weiser: A Journey to Onondaga, 1750

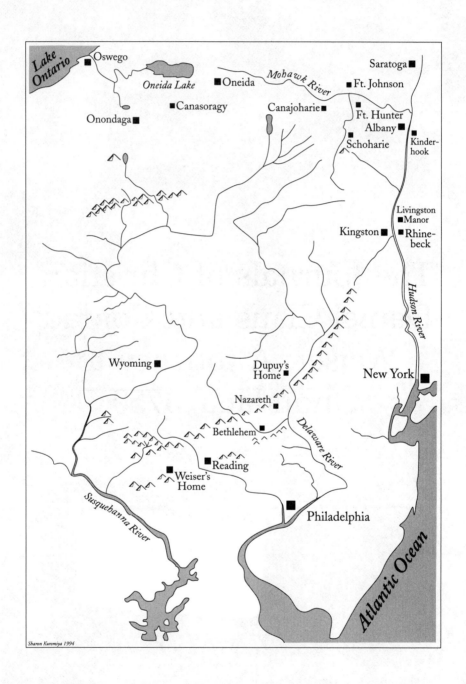

Lake Ontario

Oswego ■

Oneida Lake

Oneida ■

Mohawk River

Saratoga ■

Ft. Johnson ■

■ Canasoragy

Canajoharie ■

Onondaga ■

Ft. Hunter ■
Albany ■

Schoharie

Kinder-
hook ■

Livingston
■ Manor

Kingston ■   ■ Rhine-
beck

Hudson River

Wyoming ■

Dupuy's
Home ■

New York ■

Nazareth ■

Bethlehem ■

Delaware River

Reading ■

Weiser's ■
Home

Philadelphia ■

Susquehanna River

Atlantic Ocean

Sharon Kuromiya 1994

TRANSACTIONS

of the

American Philosophical Society

Held at Philadelphia for Promoting Useful Knowledge

VOLUME 84, Pt. 2

The Journals of Christian Daniel Claus and Conrad Weiser: A Journey to Onondaga, 1750

Translated and Edited by Helga Doblin and William A. Starna

THE AMERICAN PHILOSOPHICAL SOCIETY

Independence Square, Philadelphia

Library of Congress Catalog
Card Number 94-70105
International Standard Book Number 0-87169-842-0
US ISSN 0065-9746

CONTENTS

Photo: Luc Chartier, (ANQ)

ACKNOWLEDGMENTS

First and foremost, we would like to express our gratitude to Pierre-Louis Lapointe of the Archives nationales du Québec, Sainte-Foy, who led us to the Weiser-Claus journals. He also arranged for the reproduction of the photographic plates that accompany the text and located for us the portrait of Claus. Permission to publish the journals was kindly granted by Murielle Doyle of the Archives. Sylviane Dubois of the Literary and Historical Society of Quebec furnished additional information on the journals' provenance.

We are indebted to Charles T. Gehring, The New Netherland Project, New York State Library, and Corinna Dally-Starna for their assistance in transcribing and interpreting portions of the text.

The following individuals read parts of the early drafts of the manuscript, offering constructive criticisms and helpful comments: The Reverend Frederick S. Weiser; Wanda Burch, Johnson Hall State Historic Site; Bruce Naramore, Clermont State Historic Site.

Gunther Michelson and Hanni Woodbury gave us their expert assessment of the Iroquoian language entries. Stefan Bielinski, Colonial Albany Social History Project, identified a number of the individuals mentioned by Claus while traveling through the Albany region.

Other help in our editing of the journals came from Peter Christoph, New York State Library; George Hamell, New York State Museum; Dr. Krimm, Hauptstaatsarchiv, Stuttgart; Currie Marr, SUNY Oneonta; Jill Sweet, Skidmore College; and Kay Verrilli, Starr Library, Rhinebeck, New York. The map was designed by Sharon Kuromiya and produced by the Publications Department, Suny Oneonta, Barbara Paugh, director. Thank you all.

PREFACE

The circumstances that led to the publication of these journals merit consideration inasmuch as they prove, without a shadow of a doubt, that an archivist's life is full of surprises. When we met Professor Helga Doblin in August of 1990 and showed her the original Weiser-Claus journals, we were far from thinking that it would lead to their translation, critical edition, and publication by the American Philosophical Society. We simply drew Professor Doblin's attention to the German text in the manuscript. She, in turn, brought the manuscript and her translation of the German to the attention of Professor William A. Starna, who assessed the journals' significance as a previously unknown source concerning an important period of Indian-white relations in the American colonies.

The Archives nationales du Québec purchased the original manuscript from the Literary and Historical Society of Quebec in 1942. The Society had probably acquired it in the second half of the nineteenth century, at a time when it was active in the field of archives. How it came into their hands is, however, next to impossible to establish. Most of the Claus Family Papers were acquired by the National Archives of Canada in 1883. The journals must have been originally part of that collection.

This publication is a reminder of the importance of close cooperation between archives and universities in the field of historical research. We personally believe that university departments that use archives should have closer organic links with archival institutions and archivists. Faculty members and students should be more actively engaged in research using archival sources and professional archivists should be called upon to exchange information on a regular basis with historians, anthropologists, and other users of original manuscripts and primary records. Then and only then shall we learn from one another regarding research hypotheses, problems, sources, and perspective.

Pierre-Louis Lapointe
Archivist and Historian
Archives nationales du Québec
July 16, 1993

INTRODUCTION

In February 1750, Thomas Lee, the president of the Virginia Council, wrote a letter to Conrad Weiser, his good friend from the Lancaster Treaty days. In the exchange of correspondence that followed, Lee asked Weiser, the experienced and influential Indian agent, to be a part of his ambitious proposal to unite the English colonies with the Six Nations. After discussing Lee's plan with the governor of Pennsylvania, Weiser, as he had done many times before, prepared to travel to Onondaga, deep in Iroquois country.

Weiser's principal task at Onondaga was to invite Iroquois representatives to a council at Fredericksburg, where they would be addressed by Lee about issues of "Importance and altogether for the Good of the Publick, especially of the Six Nations." They would also receive the presents promised to them at Lancaster in 1744. However, what Weiser would not fully admit to the Iroquois, although they voiced their suspicions, was that the Catawbas would be at Fredericksburg as well. There, Lee hoped to negotiate a peace between these two adversaries, "which has never been done yet."

For over fifty years the Iroquois and Catawbas had carried out a bitter and deadly campaign of raids and reprisals against one another, the reasons for which are lost in time. Throughout, the Iroquois had been the aggressors, sending war parties into the Carolina piedmont in search of villages to raid and prisoners to take. In turn, the Catawbas, needing a foe of their own, as historian James Merrell has observed, responded to the Iroquois in kind. At least, that is how it went for many years.

By the mid-eighteenth century, the Catawbas, besieged by their enemies and the ravages of disease, and under duress from white settlement in their hunting territories that drove away needed game animals, seemed ready for peace. Certainly the Iroquois saw them as a "most conquered enemy," despite the Catawbas' vow that, even after death "their very bones shall fight."

Whatever the circumstances, Weiser was unable to convince the Iroquois to attend Lee's council, and the Iroquois' request to meet instead at Albany, a signal of their own fear to venture into enemy territory, was rebuffed. Weiser returned home and reported his failure to Lee.

Weiser's mission to Onondaga may have been doomed from the start. While in the Mohawk Valley, he learned that South Carolina's Governor Glen had written to Governor Clinton of New York, requesting his assistance in arranging a peace between the Iroquois and Catawbas. Clinton had placed the matter in the hands of Sir William Johnson, a decision to which Weiser, probably reluctantly, deferred. Once at Onondaga, Weiser was told of the "several private Conferences" the Moravian Bishop John Cammerhoff had "in the Bushes" with a certain chief, an intrigue that seems to have troubled him.

Making matters much worse, however, was the unexpected death of Canasatego, Weiser's old ally and a powerful, pro-English Onondaga chief, two days before Weiser arrived at Onondaga. His replacement was Tohaswuchdioony, a Roman Catholic sympathetic to the French.

• • •

On a June afternoon in 1750, Weiser took a room in a "Mr. Keppele's" tavern in Philadelphia where he was attending to some business. He was greeted there by another lodger, twenty-two-year-old Christian Daniel Claus, whom he had met briefly the previous winter. Weiser had learned then that Claus was stranded in the city after having lost a considerable sum of money in an investment scheme concocted by a fellow German and "a Clergyman's Son." Sympathetic to Claus's predicament, Weiser invited him to join the party traveling to Onondaga.

Weiser and Claus both came from the state of Württemberg in Germany. Claus was born into a prominent and prosperous family and was well educated. Weiser's family, on the other hand, had settled in the small farming community of Gross Aspach, where his father, after serving in the army, worked as a baker. Born in 1696, Weiser attended the village school for a time, at least until his family emigrated to England in 1709. In June of the following year, he, along with hundreds of other Palatine Germans, landed in America. Claus, born in 1727, did not arrive in America until 1749, at a time when Weiser had already been working his second farm, this one in Tulpehocken, Pennsylvania, for twenty years.

"A great friendship ensued" from their journey, and upon their return from Onondaga, Weiser introduced Claus to Pennsylvania's governor, James Hamilton. Hamilton encouraged Claus to return to "the Mohawk Town at Fort Hunter & endeavour to improve in & acquire the Iroquois Language as much as he could." There, he struck up a friendship with Sir William Johnson.

Claus took full advantage of his situation, becoming fluent in Mohawk and learning from Johnson's considerable experience in Indian affairs. In 1755 he was made a lieutenant in the Indian department and a deputy secretary of Indian affairs in the colony. His patron and friend Conrad Weiser died in 1760. In 1762, Claus married Johnson's daughter, Ann (Nancy). He went on to distinguish himself as an interpreter and British Indian agent, and died in Britain in 1787.

· · ·

Weiser and Claus's journey would take them from Tulpehocken and Reading, northwest to the Delaware, where they followed the Shawangunk mountains into northern New Jersey, entering the Hudson Valley near Kingston. From here they proceeded north to Albany, and then west into the Mohawk Valley to Onondaga. They returned through the Schoharie Valley, traveling overland to Catskill, and then south along the Hudson and the Delaware and home.

· · ·

The journals of Weiser and Claus are contained in a small volume of two hundred pages, seventy of which are blank. Bound in brown leather, the booklet measures 17.5 cm X 11.5 cm X 3 cm The original is in the collections of the Archives nationales du Québec at Sainte-Foy, and is accessioned as the Weiser-Claus Journal, Quebec Literary and Historical Society Collection, Centre d'Archives de Québec et de Chaudière-Appalaches, Archives nationales du Québec, call number ANQ-03Q, P450/7.

Besides the journals, the volume contains prayers in English, the Christian creed in Mohawk, German travel songs, assorted memoranda, religious Latin and French poetry, the beginning translation of the French epos *Télémaque*, a brief story about a Duke of Argyle, some laundry lists, writing exercises, a little love poetry, and expense accounts, one from the journey and the other of an unknown German wine merchant, possibly living in Philadelphia. Finally, there is an incomplete Mohawk-German dictionary.

In order to bring the main topic into focus, we have changed the original order of the entries in the manuscript by first presenting the journals of Claus and Weiser. These are followed by portions of the material remaining that bear directly on the journey itself. We have excluded extraneous matters such as the prayers, the accounts of the wine merchant, and the Latin, French, and English poetry.

Entries in the volume that we present here are written in English and German, the latter in German script. Words in the Iroquoian and French languages are in Latin script. The two journals were written by Weiser and Claus respectively. The Mohawk-German word list, "The Creed," the "Memorandum at Onondaga," the record of traveling expenses, a list of personal items, and several isolated statements, are Claus's. The "Extraord[inary] Memor[andum]," the "Memorandum to Onondaga," and "news at onontago," are Weiser's.

In the transliteration and translation of the German, linguistic errors and slips have been silently corrected. To insure authenticity, however, occasional attempts at clarification have been placed in brackets. This was also done in transcribing Weiser's English. As Claus's sentence constructions and punctuation marks obscure the meaning of the text at times, we have substituted their modern usage to avoid any misunderstandings.

The transcriptions from English are entirely verbatim, with no corrections and only limited comment. We followed this practice because Weiser later wrote an official report and several memoranda and letters from what are essentially his field notes, here in the form of journal entries. Thus, this is one of those rare and informative instances in history where it is possible to compare first drafts with final reports.

In Claus's journal, the spelling of geographical and European personal names, with some exceptions, follow present-day conventions. Latin terms used in the text are in capital letters. Throughout, our explanatory comments are within brackets and italicized.

[The journal of Christian Daniel Claus, translated from the German, begins here. Passages and words that were written in English are underlined.]

DIC CUR HIC[1]

Undertaking a journey to visit strange lands can neither be censured nor praised. One knows from experience that some [journeys] have been useful to some people, harmful, at least not salutary, to others; it all depended on the frame of mind in which they were undertaken, i.e., with reasonable or foolish intentions.

The usual purpose of traveling ought to be learning to know the world, that is observing the peoples and their mores, habits and comportment and fittingly employ these observations to one's use. As for the means, some are to be considered before, some during and some after the journey.

Before starting, anyone intending to travel must on the one hand look at the condition of his mind with respect to its natural state as well as to the adroitness he has already achieved through diligence; for it is well known that there are many opportunities to learn while traveling but one can also easily make mistakes and get trapped in all kinds of vices. Therefore it is particularly useful when he is somewhat conversant in the language of those peoples whom he intends to visit. On the other hand, [he must also look] not only at the condition of his body in view of the fact that it is not advisable for everybody to go on a journey but also at the condition of his finances because in this kind of situation he must be well provided with money. Had the journey actually started, he will tend to all these things and look for a convenient opportunity to get from one place to another. Then he needs appropriate discretion with board and lodging and will have to become acquainted with the foreign people whose mores and habits he must get to know as quickly as possible. When he is at the assigned place, he will visit the things worth seeing as that is anyway his ultimate purpose and then sketch the most noteworthy into his travel book. At times it works rather well when he is provided with supportive letters of introduction. After the journey, he will have to know how in the end he can share the things he has seen and become aware of while at the same time abstain

---

[1]'Tell why you are here'.

from all the boasting and exaggeration and not start to talk about it at every opportunity to the annoyance of others.

A traveler has to pay good attention—as it recently became evident—to the name of the kingdom or empire wherever he happens to be; its name, the length and width of its borders, camps, neighbors, air, fecundity, departments, citadels, provinces, castles, market towns, rivers, lakes, bordering seas, forests, mountains, quarries, health spas and fountains, edifices, religion and mores, ceremonies and form of government; whether it is independent and duly qualified; its regents, statutes, laws, liberties, prerogatives, pretensions, code of arms, ethics, mores, habits, language, commerce and income.

When he comes to a place, be it a citadel or a market town, he must find out [:]

1.) its name, the one it had since time immemorial, and the one it carries today as well as its provenance.

2.) The place's origin, who had built it, who enlarged and who renovated it.   .

3.) The location, where it is situated, how it is built and what form it has. Whether the air is healthy, whether the soil fertile, whether there are mountains, valleys, forests, woods as yet extant; the rivers that flow either nearby or parallel to or right through, the ocean or the lake on which it lies.

4.) The existing sacred buildings that belong to the community, i.e., the cathedral, the minster, churches, monasteries, convents, chapels, schools, hospitals, orphanages and asylums or else the secular such as the palace, castles, brothels, citadels, ports, fortifications, walls, gates, squares, towers, market, city hall, arsenal, department stores, granaries, custom houses, or [those belonging to] private persons, that contain statues, paintings, garden fountains, rarities, collection of coins or exhibition of art.

5.) As for the inhabitants, their religion, churches, character, rites, the regime, the form of government, law and order, schools, academies, gymnasiums, village schools and whatever belongs to them, the habits, customs, mores, economy, clothing, food, arts, skill in the handling of guns, life style and so forth.

With this, heightened circumspection is wanted in all places so that, as we said before, he will not bring strange vices, indecent customs and evil habits home with him but devote himself in all places conscientiously to observing what is beautiful, laudable and wholesome so that he can use those to good advantage in the future.

Philadelphia, June 23 [*sic*], 1750

The day before yesterday, i.e., Wednesday the 20th [*sic*] of this month, it happened that Mr. Conrad Weiser Esq.,[2] one of the Justices of [the] Peace in Tulpehocken, County of Lancaster, arrived in Philadelphia about 3 o'clock in the afternoon to tend to some business and took his lodging in Mr. Keppele's Tavern & Shopkeeper where I together with my brother-in-law Kreuser happened to be.[3] As we had the pleasure to speak and become acquainted with him once before, i.e., this past winter, we duly greeted him upon his arrival whereupon he immediately invited us to a glass of Rheinwein and stayed with us for a good while. But since he was as burdened with business in this city as ever, he tried to get to and accomplish the most essential. We too excused ourselves and went to our lodging. The following day after something had happened in our lodging that did more than a little harm to our honor and reputation,[4] we went to Keppele's House on Friday morning, which since our sojourn here has always shown itself a good and friendly place. The owner now shared that which had happened to us with Mr. Weiser, who was present and saw how it grieved me. We took leave very soon, however, and went home.

Several hours thereafter, 2 acquaintances visited us, who were close compatriots from Germany and had taken their lodging in the same inn, i.e., Mr. M. T. W. and F. B. They invited me to accompany them on a journey, with which Mr. Weiser had said that he had been charged by the governments[5] in Virginia regarding an ambassadorial commission to the 6 Indian Nations and to the council in Onondaga.[6] If I liked their company, I would be welcome. As he [Mr. Weiser] was pressed for time, he had asked them to invite me; otherwise he would have come himself to offer it to me. If I were willing to accept his proposal, he wanted me to come to him because he intended to talk further particulars over with me. I did not hesitate for long but went to him at once to become thoroughly informed about the true facts behind these plans. Since he confirmed all that the 2 persons had described, everything was immediately accepted by me and on my own free

---

[2]The authoritative biography on Weiser is *Conrad Weiser, 1696–1760, Friend of Colonist and Mohawk*, by Paul A. Wallace (1945).

[3]Henry Keppele, born in Treschklingen in Baden, was a merchant in Philadelphia. In 1764 he was elected to the Pennsylvania Assembly (Frederick S. Weiser, pers. comm., August 1992).

[4]Claus took the details of this incident to his grave.

[5]Here, and in two other places in his journal, Claus writes this word in French.

[6]See Wallace (1945), especially chapters 37 and 38, for the details of this commission.

will. A great friendship ensued since then because for such an opportunity he could otherwise have seen and investigated more than 1000 others. Mr. Weiser still added that if I did not wish to stay in the city, I could go to Tulpehocken until the beginning of the journey and live in his house there. I accepted this also. The next week on Thursday, June 28 I set out and arrived there the following Saturday. I spent the time with many little pastimes in the countryside and in the woods up to our departure, which occurred on Wednesday, Aug. 15. The journey was made by both of us as the immediately following journal shows in detail.

1750 Journey/DIC CUR HIC/to Onondaga

Aug.

16   Yesterday at 2 o'clock in the afternoon we began our jour-
      ney and arrived at the newly organized city of Reading in
      good time where Mr. Weiser had to deliver some things;
      he also had to negotiate the meetings that had to be an-
      nounced to the government. To describe this place a little,
      we must begin with the name Reading as mentioned
      above, which comes from a place in Old England where
      the proprietor Richard Penn[7] was supposedly born. The
      Main Street was meted out 3 years ago, to be sure, but no
      more work had been done to it until last year, i.e., [17]49
      when it was restarted, and many more bids were declared
      and also built.

      And what in time has proven to be the greatest asset was
      the Schuylkill River, its name of Indian provenance,[8]
      whose east side banks were densely populated. This river
      flowed a few miles further down into the Delaware River,
      likewise so named by the Indians, on whose banks lay
      such highly distinguished places of this province as New-
      castle, Chester and Philadelphia and which also brought
      ships coming in from foreign countries. The city was built
      in [left blank][9] and organized by the proprietor [Thomas]
      Penn.[10] Concerning the air and fertility, they were as good

----

[7]The Penn brothers, Richard, John and Thomas, the sons of William Penn, were by 1750, proprietaries of Pennsylvania.

[8]This word is Dutch: *schuyl*, 'to hide' or 'to conceal something', followed by *kill*, 'creek' (Charles T. Gehring, pers. comm., April 1992).

[9]Reading was established about 1738.

[10]Although Thomas Penn was the proprietor of Reading, Weiser was instrumental in its planning and involved in selling real estate there (Wallace 1945: 288, 336, 356).

as in any place in this province and there was no loss of good water to the sea. The inhabitants were for the most part Germans and Lutherans and as it was in the whole province, the laws were based on English laws. At 6 o'clock in the morning, we set out in good weather, traveled through the <u>Township</u> [of] Alsace and came [*The first part of Claus's journal ends abruptly here to make room for the English language journal of Conrad Weiser*].[11]

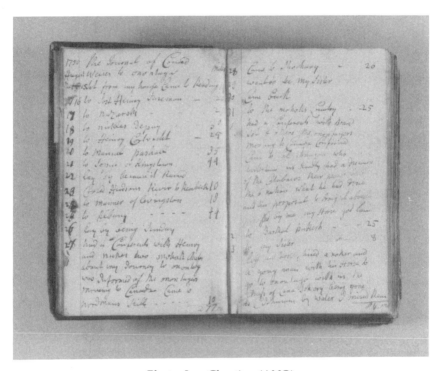

Photo: Luc Chartier, (ANQ)

1750 August	The Journal of Conrad Weiser to Onontago	miles
15	set from my house Came to Reading	14
16	to Jost Heinrich Saseman[12]	20
17	to Nazareth	27

---

[11]Weiser filed an official report, based on this journal, that is published in *Minutes of the Provincial Council of Pennsylvania from the Organization to the Termination of the Proprietary Government*,5: 470–80, hereinafter cited as MPC.

[12]"Henry Saseman in Maxatawny" (MPC: 470). Jost Henrich Sassmannshausen (anglicized to Sassmann, Sasemann, Sassaman) had emigrated from an area near Cologne, Germany, in 1721 (Frederick S. Weiser, pers. comm., August 1992).

18	to nicklas depuy[13]	30
19	to Heinry Cortrecht[14]	29
20	to Manuel pashall[15]	35
21	to Sopus or Kingstown[16]	44
22	lay by because it Rained	
23	Crosed Hudson River to Reinbeck	10
24	to Mannor of livingston	18
25	to Albany	44
26	lay by being Sunday	
27	had a Conference with Heinry and nickes, two Mohok Chiefes[17] about my Journey to onontage was Informed of the onontagers moveing to [the French in] Canada Came to nordmans Kill.[18]	10
		277m.
28	Came to Shochary[19]	26
29	went to see my sister[20]	
30	Came back	
31 1	to the mohoks Country had a Conference with Brand, Set & others.[21] The onontagers moving to Canada Confirmed. Came to Col. Johnson[22] who entertain us kindly. had a discourse of the Catabaws their peace with the 6 nations what he had done and his proposal to bring it about propossed by me[23] my Horse got lame.	25

---

[13]Wallace (1945: 305; cf. Muhlenberg 1942, 1: 247–48) identifies Nicholas Dupuy (DePuy, Depew, Dupuis, Depue, Debois) as a retired justice of the peace and the grandson of a Huguenot refugee who had come to New Amsterdam in 1662. He had purchased 3,000 acres of land from the Minisink Indians in 1727, and "was now very old" (Muhlenberg 1942, 1: 247).

[14]A Dutch Reformed preacher and a member of the consistory of Minisink and Kingston in 1744 (ERNY 4: 2843, 2862; Muhlenberg 1942, 1: 248).

[15]See note 74.

[16]Esopus. In Munsee, an Algonquian language, 'person from sopus' (Goddard 1978: 237). Today, Kingston, New York.

[17]Nicklas (Nickas) is "the Sachim and one of the proprietors of Conajoharee" (SWJP 13: 15). Heinry is Theyanoguin, Hendrick, King Hendrick, Henry Peters, etc. (ca. 1680–1755), (Jennings et al. 1985a: 253; MPC: 470).

[18]The Normans Kill.

[19]Schoharie.

[20]Claus, below, says that this person is Weiser's "half- sister," i.e., Anna Rebecca, the wife of Friederich Klein (Frederick S. Weiser, pers. comm., August 1992).

[21]Probably Brant (Canagaraduncka) (m. 1738) or Brant (Kaweghnagey) (d. 1760) (Kelsay 1984: 51–52). Seth (Otchenuchyate), the chief sachem at Schoharie (SWJP 9: 589; Jennings et al. 1985b: 650).

[22]Sir William Johnson (1715–1774), provincial and crown agent for Indian affairs.

[23]See Merrell (1987, 1989) for discussions on Iroquois-Catawba relations.

being Black Wampum Saristaquo[34] Came to
see me—the rest of the Chiefes being in
mourning did not Come the Indians seamed
to be much affected by the death of
Canasatego having lost several of their head
men these few years. Three noted men died
within a twelve month besides Canas.° he
with Toganiha & Caxhayion in pensilvania
last sumer and Solkiwanachty[35] a Chief since
his arrival from philadelphia

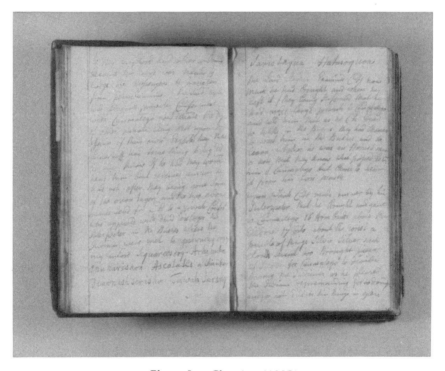

Photo: Luc Chartier, (ANQ)

11 no deputys arrived nothing was done
12 none arrived I desired to be heard tomorrow
    morning by the onontagers only they
    begged I might have patience one day longer
    my landlord & Saristaquoa told me what

---

[34]Saristagoa, an Oneida (Jennings et al. 1985b: 641; cf. MPC: 475).
[35]All three of these individuals were Onondaga chiefs: Tocanihan or Tocanyhaa (Jennings et al. 1985b: 685); Coxhayion (Wallace 1945); and Solkiwanachty or Soterwanachty
(Jennings et al. 1985b: 662).

passed between them and Mr. Camerhoff &
david Zeisberger[36] two moravians who
Came to onontago some time this sumer,
but took up lodging in another house which
gave offence to my landlord and other
Indians because his house was named to
lodge the messengers & travelers from
pensilvania. The said men had several
private Conferences with Canasatego now
deceased the deput. of other nations being
much upon for affairs of their own Expected
they that Camerhoff had something to say
did let him know If he had they would hear
him but received answer he had not. after
they being gone some of the onontagers and
the two above named send for CH[37] to a
private Confer.ˢ who appeared with david
Zeisberger his Interpreter in the Bushes[38]
where the Indians were met. to
gashwuchyoony my landlord Tequareesery,
Arhounta anuharishon, Ascotaks a Sinniker
diaoneshserisho, Tuwatsdarany, Saristaqua
Hatasoquoa[39] The said Indians Examined
CH how much he had brought and where
he left it/they being Informed that he had
made large presents to Canasatego and told
him that as he Ch. loved to talk in the
Bushes they had choosen to meet him in the
Bushes and to learn whether he was an
Honest man or not that they knew what
passed bet.ʷ him & Canasatego but Choose
to hear it from his own mouth

upon which CH made answer by his
Interpreter that he brought and gave to

---

[36]Bishop Johann Christoph Frederick Cammerhoff (1722–1751) had studied in Jena, Thu-
ringia, and in 1747 was ordered to the Moravian mission in America. David Zeisberger
(1721–1808) was a noted interpreter, translator, and student of Iroquoian languages (Goddard 1988: 698–99).

[37]Cammerhoff.

[38]"In the bushes" is a common reference to informal meetings and private discussions,
held out of council.

[39]Arhounta or Aruntyony, an Onondaga chief present at a council in Philadelphia in
1742 (Jennings et al. 1985b: 435). Ascotaaks or Ascotax, a Seneca and a signatory to a 1736
deed, also in Philadelphia (ibid.). "Sinneker," a Seneca.

Canasatego 16 Arm bands above the Elbows
17 dito about the wrist a pundle[40] of rings
silver neck cloath several two Brought pieces
of silver for Canasatego to divide among the
Indians as he pleased the Indians
repremanding for so doing and for not
diliver this things in open Counsel. he said
he had something to say to them in Counsel
also which they desired to hear he said that
he had it in Charge from Anna queen/the
Indians name of queen Ann the Ind.[s] to this
day understand the Crowned head of great
Britain/to warn the Indians not to let the
white people settle to much of their land
which would make the Indians poor and
ruin the trade and desired the Indians by a
string of Wampum which he gave them to
take notice.

by another string of wampum he desired
liberty to Erect a shmith shop on
Woyumock.[41]

then by a large Belt of Wampum he desired
leave for two men to live among them at
onontago for two years or longer till he had
the Indians language perfect and promised
that the two men shall take Care of their
affairs. he CH being asked what was the
reason that Tharaghinwagon[42] did not Come
with this message he answered Thar.[n] is of
another sort of people and no more in
favour and after our people that will learn to
speak your language Come back he will
have nothing more to do with Indians affairs
my landlord hereupon gave him the lie and
said it is in no Body power to Cut CW off

---

[40]This word is "bundle." Because of characteristics in his local dialect, Weiser did not
distinguish between voiced and voiceless stops. Thus, in English, he often wrote p for b,
and d for t, and vice versa, as did Claus on occasion.

[41]Wyoming. The Wyoming Valley and its Indian settlements were in the general area of
Wilkes-Barre, Pennsylvania, on the north branch of the Susquehanna River, in territory
controlled by the Iroquois.

[42]Weiser's Indian name, often, *Tarachawgon* 'Holder of the Heavens' (cf. Wallace 1945).

till he dies. all what you said and did is of
your own accord and our Brother onas[43]
knows nothing of it.

upon which CH made answer that he did
not Come out of his own accord but was
sent by several great men to wit
Tagerhitonly, Caniadarechcon,
Hashtwuchdioony[44] bid him to take up his
wampum and be gone, but CH insisted
upon that they should Keep them. They told
me that.

Since this CH was in the Sinniken Country
and told the Indians there that he had
bought land from Canasago at onontago and
paid him with silver truk.[45] This last article I
dont belief but it is Currantly reported at
onontago and by private Intelligance I had it
was the occassion of C.s.gos death.

The two great pieces of silver came from the
king one for the warriors the other for the
Chiefes.[46]

13   The deputies of the oneiders & Tuscaroro
      arrived before night William
                              J
      ganachquéieson[47] diwaiadáchgon,
                  Joseph
      Haruchiennunto, Candarúntie.
      dewaiudachgon is a Tuscaoror his name is
      known by the name of Capt. Helly.
      Haruchiennunt is known by the name of
      Sakawárunt.

14   held a privat with the deputies aforesaid
      about the death of Canas.° How to Condole

---

[43]The Iroquois' name for William Penn ('feather').
[44]Caniadarechcon or Ganataraykon, a Cayuga headman reported to have attended a
council with the French in 1748 (Jennings et al. 1985b: 513).
[45]"Truck," i.e., trade goods, small articles that were exchanged or bartered.
[46]This entry for September 12 does not appear in Weiser's official report. However,
Weiser's "Memorandum taken at Onondaga the 12th Sept'', 1750," is derived entirely from
what he recorded here (Wallace 1945: 313–14, 599 n 22).
[47]An Oneida.

with the onontagers and to form the speech
of us all to onontagers in order remove their
mourning to inable them to sit in Counsel. I
gave a string of Wampum of three rows & a
Belt for that purpose we all appointed
Canachqueison speaker in that affair.

About noon the Counsel meet. The
onontagers Chiefes that were present their
name Tehashwuchdioony, hatachsago,
Gechdachery and ganodu, mit das weissen
Kap,[48] beside the forenamed with
Saristaquoa ganachqueieson open the
Counsel and desired to be heard. received
answer that they were ready to hear him.
upon which he directed his discourse to the
onontagers said father we you sons to wit
the ononeiders, garuyquons[49] and
Tuscaroros also your Brother asaryquoa[50]
entered your dorr in very melonchally time
when yours Eies is most blind before for
the tears you shed and your sorrow full in
the highest degree because for the death of
the great man[51] Buried the other day. We
your sons and your Brother before named
make bold to Come near you in order to
Comfort you in your troubles and whip of
the tears from your Eies and to Clear your
throat that you may be able to speak again.
We also waganochaly, anoquushsa
Cennachagy, Clean the Cabin again or
Counsel room from what evil that might be
have occassioned the death of that great
man lately Buried.

here the speaker gave a string of Wampum
of nine rows, and gave another of the same
seiz, with a Belt of Wampum to Coffer the
grave of Canasatego.

---

[48]Incorrect German for 'with the white cap', a reference to Hendrick, also known as
White Head (Jennings et al. 1985a: 253).
[49]Cayugas (cf. MPC: 476).
[50]Iroquois name for the Governor of Virginia ('long knife').
[51]Weiser (MPC: 476–77) observes that "(a dead man's name must not be mentioned
among those People)."

After a ~~little~~ short pause, the speaker at my
request and by my direction spoke again to
the folowing purport and in my behalf.
Brethren of the six united nations to wit
digarihogon,[52] Sasgosdanagechteront,
dyiontsin Hogararow, Nittaronhaquoa
Sanunowartowans & Tuscarroro. I am sent
to your Counsel fire by your Brother
assaryquoh and what I am going to say will
be as If you heard it out of the mouth of
your Brother Assaryquoa gave a large string
of wampum. Then the speaker tooke the
large string of Wampum and said Brethren
the governor of virg.^{ia} invides you to Come
down to the town Called fridericksburg
being in virginia to a public treaty he is
directed by the great king over the sea to do
so. It will be things of great moment and to
your good that he will Transact with you he
therefore desires that you will not refuse his
invidation but Come to the treaty—gave the
string of Wampum. Then I gave a Belt of
Wampum and desired the speaker to speak
as follows
Bretheren I have kindled a Counsel fire at
fricksburg aforesaid where you may sit in
safety ~~and~~ as under a shadow of a tree to
hear to Consider and to speake to the affairs
that shall be transacted there as If you
where at your own fire at onontago gave the
Belt of wampum—
Then I gave a string of Wampum in behalf
of the Govr of pensil.^{ia} and said Brethren
the message of the governor of pensilvania
is known to me and has lodged within my
dorrs on the journey, and
~~is of great~~ I desire that you will Except of
the invidation. I find it will be to your
advantage.

---

[52]This may be Tekarihoken (Togarihoan, Degarihogan), a Mohawk sachem or civil
chief's title.

And so concluded and said that I was
resolved to turn homewords tomorrow If
they Could give me an answer this night.

I was told that I must have patience another
day to morrow I should have their answer.

by sun set the onontagers returned thanks
for the Comfortation & Condole. by a long
speech made by Tahushwuchdioony. The
Chief words was Iawu, Iawu Zinachseery[53]
and he also whipt off our tears by giving a
string of wampum to the oneiders and one
to me with the words Icanuh, Icanuh
Tissonucht loonie.[54]

     The answer of the 6 nations
Brother Asserygo we take your invidation
kindly and should be very glad to see you
but every time when we go down to see our
Brother onas I lost so many of our people &
particular last sumer we lost so many of our
people and all our head men that we left
like a people without a head and we fear
that If we go down to farr as to your
Counsel fire we will loose still more as there
is so many days Journey more to pass
through the white people. We desire
therefor that you will move your fire to
Albany. It Can Easily be done we perceive
you can come by water safe and there we
gladly hear you and receive the presents you
asked us from the King for the land our
former deputies, now old, death, assigned
you we never yet received any thing gave a
large string of Wampum.
Brother onas you dont Consider our
Circumstances in giving us encouragement
to Come to virginia when all our great men
that was down with you died by the way of
Coming up last year. It had been your duty

---

[53]This is not recognizably Onondaga or any other Iroquoian language (Hanni Woodbury, pers. comm., April 1992).
  [54]Idem.

to wasatanwâsery[55] as the gover.[n] of n.y. -
does on such occassion [*illegible word*]
wahatanásery, who shall speak with Br.
assaryquoa our great men are all death.
Your belt you gave us to take notice of your
Counsel fire we will Exchange at Albany
and give you all the satisfaction in our
power.[56]

[*Weiser's journal ends here. Claus provides the following narrative, written in German, one that was recorded initially by Weiser in English.*]

Memorandum at Onondaga

One evening, two Indians had a dispute about religion; one professed the English [Anglican] the other the Roman Catholic. Mr. Weiser appended this dispute to his journal (and I later translated it into German).[57] To wit:

Ganachquajéson, one of the Indian deputies, who was a protestant convert, had a discussion with one by the name of Jahaswuichdiuuny, with whom we stayed and [who professed] the Roman religion. He is now the most sublime or king. Jahaswuichdiuuny asked Ganachquajéson whether it was true that such and such an Indian (he named him) had quite desperately uttered, that he would have to go to hell after his death and live with the devils. Ganach. replied that the man had [indeed] said so but he had been very sick having had restiveness and great temptations to his soul in firmly insisting on his point of view and it had been lasting a good while but in the end he [the man] had become a bit doubtful.

Jahas. said: When [in spite of] being baptised you will have to go to hell, what good is your baptism? For he who is baptized by

---

[55]This looks like the name Wahanatseary, a Seneca present at the Albany Conference of August 6, 1754 (Jennings et al. 1985b: 701). However, the context of the word suggests that it is an Indian name for, or a reference to, the governor of New York. Customarily, New York and its governor were referred to as Corlaer.

[56]Weiser's official report continues from here (cf. MPC: 478–80).

[57]Weiser's account of this exchange is not found in his journal or official report. It appears instead in a separate document held by the Historical Society of Pennsylvania (cf. Wallace 1945: 311–13, 599 n. 20). Claus's translation of Weiser's English into German is retranslated here into English.

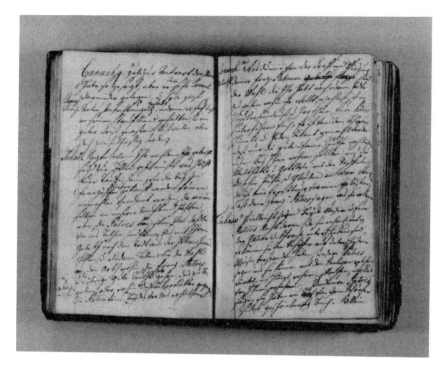

Photo: Luc Chartier, (ANQ)

the two French priests, will never be damned. We ourselves should hold to our covenant of baptism but the Fathers[58] report that they pray for us and after death get us out of hell with their prayers and then we have the choice to go either to the place where the French Fathers and the other good people move or where our forefathers went. The Fathers are able to obtain either for us.

Ganach: What you are telling me about prayer, the power and effect of your French Fathers and your choice to go where you want to after your death, is a misunderstanding. Your Fathers mislead you. It has been made known by the Creator of heaven and earth that after this life none but the good and pious people shall live with Him and the evildoers and godless, those who are without repentance and faith in Jesus Christ, will stay with the devils. There is no salvation for a bad [person]. Let your Fathers say what they want.

---

[58]In the original, Claus wrote "Father" in Latin. However, like the good Latin scholar he was, Claus had changed the nominative PATER, 'Father', to the different Latin cases the German syntax demanded.

Jahas: Perhaps both our and your Fathers are right. As they are different in nation and language, they may have understood the Creator in a different way. Our Fathers tell us that they are able to talk to the blessed who really reside in heaven and learn everything from them; and your Fathers say that they have a book that was written by the Creator Himself. But our Fathers do not want to grant them that but say that they have the original of that book and yours have nothing but the copy, written by someone who did not even understand it correctly.

Ganach: The book about which we are speaking is the very same among all the nations and our Fathers have the same that yours have, which all admitted. There is no difference but that your Fathers say they can talk with the souls that reside in heaven. It is they that cause all the misfortune and error for they teach you lies, which run counter to the things that are written in that book by the Creator Himself; this is also the reason why your French Fathers do not want to let the common people have these books lest their fraud might be discovered.

Jahas: I admit that the French Fathers take us in at times. I once asked my Fathers, whether I would be forced to go to heaven where the Fathers and all the good people went or not? He told me no. I asked another one to search the heavens whether my grandfather was there and he promised to do that for me; he told me the other day that he had seen him there. Thereupon I held it up to him how he [my grandfather] had been able to get in there in spite of having hated the French Fathers and their religion like poison. He once had even caught a Father and taken him to Onondaga so that he [the Father] could be burnt to ashes alive; he [the grandfather] commanded his children and grandchildren to kill the French Fathers whenever they could get them into their power. Thereupon the French Father answered that he had perhaps mistaken the person and said he wanted to look once more; when I visited him a few days later, he reported to me that he had indeed made a mistake as the person whom he had taken to be my grandfather, had really been my father's grandfather; my grandfather was in hell. I told him he was a liar as I was certain that my great-grandfather had entered the blessed land where the Indian forefathers had gone after their death. And this is the place, Brother Ganachquajéson, where I also wish to go and nowhere else. We are being taken in by the white men in this world and if we do not pay attention, they will make us their slaves.

Ganach: Although I am unable to inform you thoroughly about the doctrine of our Father, I am much amused to hear from you that you would rather go to our forefathers than to the place where the French Fathers go.[59]

[*Claus's journal resumes here.*] to describe the Provinces of New York and [New] Jersey and not to forget the rivers where they originate, where they fall into the ocean, what sort of metal[60] they have in them, what kind of fish live there. At 2 o'clock in the afternoon to Reading from Tulpehocken in good weather; 13 miles; [to] carpenter Rugbry.

To the smith Heinrich Schneider from there; Müller showed us the way via the Fox Plantation; from there to Trible Piece[61] in Maxatowny County, Jeriob had stones.[62] We rode 7 miles astray in the rain and got to Debald[63] Meyer [?] and spent the night at Jost Heinrich Sassmann.[64] Early in the morning, we rode another 31 miles in fog and dismal weather and came to Peter Drepler, an old acquaintance of Mr. Weiser. There we found an acquaintance from Virginia, a traveling companion, who had been following us on our way for the past 40 miles, and came to the Zinzendorf village of Bethlehem[65] where Bishop Cammerhoff invited us to a cup of coffee and a pipe of tobacco. The whole night long, he told us of his journeys to the Indians, that he had undertaken with his brother and that had been rather important.[66] During the same night a Mr. M. T. came to us, who intended to go to Esopus;[67] we left Bethlehem around 4 o'clock in the afternoon and came to Nazareth, likewise a Zinzendorf place where we met several acquaintances of Mr. Weiser. From there we still rode 2 ½ miles to a German innkeeper, by the name of Favour [*sic*], where we spent the night. From Sassmann we had covered 30 miles up to here during the past days. In the morning we rode 6 miles in good weather and time and reached the so-called Blue Mountains,

---

[59]See Wallace (1945: 311–13) on this debate.

[60]Claus may be using the word "metal" to mean "ore," or possibly as a reference to stone used to make roads that could be drawn from river beds.

[61]This may be Johann Jacob Dreibelbiss (d. 1761), a wealthy farmer living in Richmond Township in the Maxatawny area (Frederick S. Weiser, pers. comm., August 1992).

[62]Jeriob is presumably Claus's horse, who had picked up stones or gravel in his hooves.

[63]A possible reference to the family name Dewalt (Frederick S. Weiser, pers. comm., August 1992).

[64]See note 12.

[65]"Zinzendorf," after Nikolaus Ludwig Count von Zinzendorf (1700–1760), founder of the *Herrnhuter Brudergemeinde* 'community of brethren at Herrnhut', and the Moravian church in America; thus, a Moravian village (Gollin 1967).

[66]The visit that Bishop Cammerhoff and his "brother," David Zeisberger, had just paid to the Onondagas and others of the five Iroquois nations, would figure importantly in Weiser's upcoming negotiations there, as he would soon learn (Beauchamp 1916: 24–112; cf. Wallace 1945).

[67]The Reverend Henry Melchior Mühlenberg (1711–1787) also joined Weiser and Claus at Bethlehem, and traveled with them to Rhinebeck. He was Weiser's son-in-law (Muhlenberg 1942, 1: 246).

which are 15 miles wide and have gotten their name from the many stony roads. In spite of having to lead the horses for several miles because of the stony roads, we progressed rather well and after crossing the mountains[68] we saw the Delaware River, which was still rather narrow here. We took the midday meal at the tenant of the Samuel Debois[69] Plantation of which I still have pleasant and beautiful memories with their 3000 acres of summer and winter fruit. The owner Debois and his father Peter were both present and when the latter heard that Mr. Weiser was here, he was very happy and very friendly, welcoming us warmly since he had been a good friend of the latter's father. He soon rode with us to his own plantation, from where we had a beautiful view as it lay on a mountain, and the Delaware River flowed by down below.[70] Since we had covered 30 miles in the past days, he persuaded us to spend the night and we were very well entertained. Having covered 6 miles after an early breakfast we were taken over the Delaware where we left Pennsylvania and continued our way from Walpack[71] on in the Province of New Jersey in warm weather on Wednesday [sic]; we took our midday meal at a North-German innkeeper by the name of Rosenkranz. As it was Sunday, we did not continue for more than 8 ½ miles and had our lodging with Heinrich Cortrecht, another North-German. We may pass over in silence that, as long as we traveled along the Delaware, which was 50 miles long, I could not wish for a more pleasant region, more fertile land and better roads.

On Monday the 20th of Aug., we continued our journey in cool weather (it had rained the night before) and in good time and arrived at Stewart [?] Scout Major a [?] Justice [?] Depuy at noon.[72] He handled the flute very nicely. We eagerly accepted the invitation for the midday meal and when after much preparation it appeared on the table, we saw quite strange dishes, which had been prepared in our honor. The meal consisted of bear meat and—as they called it—squash, a kind of pumpkin of subtle consistency. We had to appreciate it as an honor and ate of it with hearty yet forced appetite. At the end, we were even urged to take in several spoonfuls of bear fat, which without doing you

---

[68]Wallace (1945: 305) suggests that the party crossed these mountains, the Blue Mountains or Kittatinny Hills, through Tat's Gap.

[69]Weiser writes Depue (MPC: 470) and depuy (see note 13).

[70]The plantation was at present-day Shawnee, Pennsylvania (Wallace 1945: 305).

[71]In Monroe County, Pennsylvania.

[72]Wallace (1945: 305) identifies this man as Major DuPuy. Mühlenberg (1942, 1: 248) adds that he was a "prominent Dutch justice of the peace and a major of the militia of the province [of New York] . . . and an old acquaintance of Mr. Weiser." "Scout" may be schout, 'sheriff', in Dutch,

any harm were supposed to be good for your health. But to him who had never seen much less eaten it, it did taste neither like veal nor another such roast. We thanked our host and continued on our way. When we had traveled in the forest for about 10 miles, I saw a black bear jump over the road about 50 or 60 paces from us and when he had gotten away beyond the range of a bullet, he placed himself on an old stump, turned around and looked at us. He did not stay for long, however, but continued his way in the bush. Since it began to get dark, we noticed a fire in the bush. As we approached, we discovered an Indian hut.[73] We asked for the way to the next house, lit a pipe of tobacco and reached a house in which Emanuel Basalesh lived, whose father had been a Spaniard. He pretended to be a <u>tabern keeper</u> and be so rated by the North-German appraisers but according to the service we received from him, his business should be closed for life by an act of Parliament. Sitting on his chair with that arrogant Spanish mien he could not serve us anything but dram and water. After we had taken a little of it, he showed us our resting-place on the floor where he had spread a couple of hard skins; and with all this harsh treatment we had to feed his fleas. We strove to get rid of him as soon as possible and on the 21st of this month early in the morning we hastily rode away in good weather and bright sunshine to look for the next house where we might get breakfast.[74] Soon thereafter we came upon another so-called innkeeper, who ordered a raccoon or a badger readied for us in a hurry, which tasted quite good.[75] In the meantime it must have at least astounded my stomach to digest the meat of 2 animals so antipathetic to each other in so short a time. At noon we came to the New York village of Mombaccus[76] where we stopped and took our meal at a Gerhard de Witt. Taking the road to Esopus from there, we came one mile before Esopus through a place called Murmel[77] and very close to Esopus through the small settlement of Hurley. This entire day we found many houses as close as a quarter of a mile from each other, and traveling there was

---

[73]"[W]e also met several wild Indians," with whom Weiser spoke (Muhlenberg 1942, 1: 248).

[74]Weiser writes this name Paschal (MPC: 470) and Pashall (see text at note 15). Mühlenberg (1942, 1: 248) describes him as "a Spaniard because his father had come into this country as a Spanish prisoner, married a Dutch woman, and begot this son." Like Claus's, his portrayal is unflattering, remarking that "Spanish pompousness and Dutch rudeness had combined in this man."

[75]"At an inn we were fed on *raccoons*, the American fox or badger, and pumpkins" (Muhlenberg 1942, 1: 248).

[76]In the town of Rochester, Ulster County, New York.

[77]Also Marbletown or Marmel.

very pleasant. After covering 40 miles on this day, we safely arrived in Esopus alias Kingstown in the evening and took our
lodging with a North-German by the name of Cornelius
Elmendorph.[78] We intended to continue our journey early the
following morning but were prevented by a heavy rain that had
started that night and continued the entire day following, which
was Wednesday. We therefore took the opportunity to look
around a bit in this place [*two words illegible*]. We wanted first of
all to pay a visit to the clergyman of this settlement, whose name
Mancius[79] must have originated from the Northern German region of [Hesse-] Nassau. But since he was not at home but in
Rhinebeck on church business, we did not stop there for long but
looked around a little further in the place where in short we saw
and heard the following: First of all to explain its name, which in
English is Kingstown, in German *Königsstadt* and has been so
called when New York came to England; Esopus, however, is an
Indian name and was given to the place when it became settled.
It was built by the Dutch and being located on a pleasant plain
was still daily being expanded and restored. The streets were
rather evenly laid out so that the air should be healthy around
there. Passing by the cemetery, I was therefore strengthened in
my supposition as I could not find a single fresh grave. I have also
been told and seen for myself that most people there lived to a
ripe old age.

The place was not at all lacking in fertility and everything
planted there grew in abundance, most of all Indian corn. About
one mile from there a river called [*left blank*][80] was flowing by and
two miles further, the North or Hudson River was following its
course. No particular edifices were in sight, and the houses were
built in North-German style. As for the inhabitants, they were all
Low-Germans, the religion was Dutch-Reformed and the clergy
depended on the synod in Amsterdam [Holland]. The form of
government was English and so were the laws and regulations.
Otherwise the habits, mores and life style were Dutch and who-
ever was not willing to eat roasted corn, should not expect too
much.[81]

[78]Cornelius Elmendorph, Jr., was a member of the church of Kingston in 1766 (ERNY 6: 4040).
[79]The Reverend George Wilhelmus Mancius was associate Dominie in the Dutch Reformed Church in Kingston at the time of Claus's visit (ERNY passim; cf. Muhlenberg
1942, 1: 331).
[80]Either the Esopus or Rondout creek.
[81]Claus appears to be suggesting that accommodations among the Dutch in this area
were rather simple, if not meager, and therefore, one "should not expect too much."

On Thursday, the 23rd, when the weather had cleared up, we departed from Esopus early and were to be transported to Rhinebeck by a New England company. Thus, 2 miles from Esopus, we embarked on a ferry with [our] 4 horses and sailed across the large Hudson River, which having been joined there by the Waalen Creek,[82] was expanded to 2 full miles. We came to Rhinebeck so called later although the Indians had originally given it an Indian name. The houses were somewhat spread apart and a region of *[left blank]* miles was also called by the same name; we passed by the Dutch-Reformed Church and saw a number of people having assembled there. When we inquired after the reason, we were told that Mr. Mancius from Esopus was to preach there. We, however, hastened to the Lutheran preacher, a Mr. Hartwick[83] from Halle in Saxony, who came regularly and whose residence could thus not be far away. We went in the direction indicated up to a X X.[84] Since we were not immediately able to get in contact with him, Mr. Weiser thought it wise to go to the church mentioned before and listen to a sermon by Dni [Dominie] Mancius interpreting a text from the B[ook] of Kings, Chap[ter] V, which he explained very well. After the service was ended, we waited for the clergyman to give him our compliments; he accepted them very graciously and invited us for the midday meal. We excused ourselves on account of Mr. Hartwick, who was presently expected. He [Mancius] accepted it but was also agreeable to continue talking with Mr. Hartwick present. We therefore turned around toward Mr. Hartwick's lodgingl[85] but were intercepted on the way and invited into the house of one of Mr. Weiser's neighbors, Peter Zipperlin,[86] and kept there for the noon meal. Having finished the meal, we hastened to get to the house mentioned a few times before. When we arrived, Dominie Mancius had gotten there before us; we greeted Pastor Hartwick, sat down and various discourses ensued. Among others we complained about the bad comportment of two clergymen, who were incognito staying in this region. One of them was Lutheran and

---

[82]The Walkill or Valkill. In 1769, Richard Smith (1906: 75– 76) observed that the Walkill had two or three houses at its mouth and that trade was carried out aboard six or seven sloops apparently anchored there. The creek empties into the Hudson from the east bank, about two miles south of Kingston.

[83]John Christopher Hartwick (Johann Christoph Hartwig) a Lutheran minister, was born in Thüringen in 1714 and died at Clermont, Livingston Manor, in 1796 (Glatfelter 1980: 52).

[84]This may indicate a signpost or a crossroads.

[85]Hartwick lived in Rhinebeck (Muhlenberg 1942, 1: 248).

[86]Peter Zipperlin (Zipperli, Cipperly, Sipperle) (1725–1795), resided at East Camp (Jones 1985, 2: 1143). See note 90.

passed himself off for a prince of the House of Württemberg and really carried the name of Ludwig Carl Rudolph Prinz von Württemberg;[87] but he was continually drunk and because of indecent acts unbecoming a clergyman he was withdrawn [from active service]. Yet he liked to tell that the minute his activities had been discovered in the provinces, he was just about able to escape. As I have heard myself from reasonable people, however, he was apt to deliver good sermons as often as four times a day. It would be altogether too much to cite his many and well practiced methods but so as to present at least some idea of their nature, it was left up to the Christian church [to make them available for perusal]. To make a few short comments about the evil deeds of the other, a reformed preacher by the name of Schnurren:[88] he had to abscond from Pennsylvania because of fornication and excessive drinking. As he had taken refuge here all by himself, some information about his [past] comportment was gathered and the church was closed to him. By the way, this region is also provided with a would-be Doctor of Medicine, more endowed with naiveté than craftiness. VIDE SUPRA.[89]

Thus our journey was not longer than 6 miles today because for one, ever since Bethlehem, we had to depend on our good traveling companion Pastor Mühlenberg and secondly because Mr. Weiser still had some old acquaintances here. On the following day, the 24th of this [month], we had intended to set out on our journey much earlier but when Mr. Mühlenberg and Mr. Hartwick decided to accompany us a little on the way, our plan was somewhat delayed and thus we started as late as 8 o'clock in the morning. After 12 miles, we came to a region, which was called "the Camp,"[90] a name that originated with the first Germans, who had come here; for they had to camp the first winter in tents that had been made out of tree barks. This happened about 40 years ago and Mr. Weiser and his parents had also been present then and given the place its name. There we stopped at a North-German innkeeper by the name of Philip

---

[87]An inquiry conducted by the Staatsarchiv Württemberg in 1883 concluded that this "irregular" Lutheran minister was an imposter (Dr. Krimm, Hauptstaatsarchiv Stuttgart, pers. comm., 12 May 1992; cf. Muhlenberg 1942, 1: 249).

[88]Casper Lewis Schnorr, a former Roman Catholic, was born near Münster in Westphalia. Described by Mühlenberg (1942, 1: 154) as "a wanton sinner," he is said to have disappeared sometime after 1748 (Glatfelter 1980: 121–22).

[89]'See above'. Ludwig Carl Rudolph also claimed to be a doctor of medicine (Glatfelter 1980: 113).

[90]This was East Camp, in the vicinity of Germantown and Cheviot, New York. A place called West Camp was located directly across the Hudson River, north of Saugerties.

Photo: Luc Chartier, (ANQ)

Schumacher[91] and ordered a midday meal, however it might turn
out. In the meantime, Mr. Weiser visited several good friends,
among them also a *[left blank]* Kurtz, relative of Mr. Curtis.[92]
Thereupon we hastened to eat and were served in an upper, quite
pleasant room. While eating the dessert, I was reminded of the
perfect harvest meals we used to enjoy in Germany; for they
[here] presented apples, pears and in between them the most
beautiful and noble grapes, which were raised in the near vege-
table garden. An ingenious poet could have taken the opportunity to express his ideas about the view and the region for we had
before us the very high so-called Catskill mountains, on the highest of which there was a very large lake. There were also trees of
a special kind, which produced such aromatic sap that it was
called balm of Gilead.[93] For a quart bottle, you paid a pistol[94] in

---

[91]Also Shoemaker. An elder or deacon of the Germantown Lutheran Church in 1741
(Jones 1985, 2: 935).

[92]Kurtz may be Captain Johan Frederick Kortz (b. 1730), who commanded a company of
troops at East Camp in 1767 (Jones 1985, 1: 509).

[93]A fragrant resin extracted from the balsam fir, *Abies balsamea*; after Gilead, a region of
ancient Palestine known for its aromatic balms.

the pharmacy. The sap was collected in the following way: when bright little blisters showed on the bark of the trees, they were stunted and were of various white [colors]; then they [the workers] first let 10 or 12 drops [from each tree] fall [in a container]. After a certain time when these were all collected and no risk was perceived, they examined them. Down, close to the mountains, the large North River[95] flowed by and on the other side of the river [we saw] the most beautifully cultivated fields with all kind of fruits. We stopped full of surprise, smoked a pipe of tobacco before the horses were readied again. Thereupon we mounted and after six miles reached a place, which they called the Mannor.[96] This was as much as a freehold estate[97] in Germany and consisted of a large acreage of land lying near the Hudson River, on which the manor, some farms, mills, also a brewery and many other buildings [were standing]. The owner[98] was called Lord of the Mannor by the English, which is as much as Baron[99] in German, for he did not need to do much for the King. He had to order the punishments over the lower as well as the higher jurisdiction within his borders so that his grandfather[100] PROPERA AUTORITATE[101] had ordered a niger [sic] hanged. We paid this gentleman a visit, and when he learned that it was Mr. Weiser, he invited us to a glass of wine and a pipe of tobacco, which we accepted. Having asked about and learning of Mr. Weiser's office and diplomatic mission to the 6 Nations, he admired the care with which the governments [of] Penns[ylvania], Virg[inia] and Maryl[and] handled the Indian affairs. On the other hand, he complained about the indolence of the New Yorkers. He also assured us that he was recently informed that the French in Canada paid meticulous attention to this and tried to bring the English Indians to their side through all kind of intrigues. He had also received credible information that they [the French] presented them [the English Indians] with bordered clothes,[102] since they

---

[94]Any old European gold piece having the value of the Spanish coin, the *pistole*; thus, something expensive.

[95]The Hudson.

[96]The Manor of Livingston, a vast holding of some 160,000 acres of land, obtained by Robert Livingston (1654–1728), first lord of the manor, during the administration of Governor Thomas Dongan. Much of the land was let out to tenant farmers (Leder 1956: 6).

[97]German, *Gut*.

[98]Robert Livingston, Jr. (1708–1790), third lord of the manor.

[99]German, *Freiherr*.

[100]Robert Livingston.

[101]'Based on proper authority'.

[102]By "bordered clothes," Claus might be suggesting material with lace or brocade trim. Weiser (MPC: 475) writes "laced with Silver and Gold."

used to cover their bodies with nothing but woolen blankets before, and other gifts, and offered them to live in a boyd [?]; it had really gotten to the point that some families had moved to the French region.

It began to get dark and Mr. Mühlb. and Hartw., who had decided to accompany us up to here, now wanted to take the road to Rhinebeck again. We intended to continue our journey, but the gentleman, who writes his name Loewenstein,[103] did not allow it but persuaded us to spend the night in his house.[104] He inquired about this and that from Mr. Weiser. I, however, looked a little around in front of the house and went down to the water[105] where a small frigate[106] was being built for him; in general, I could perceive that the man [our host] managed a large business. Then workers, day laborers and servants were called to dinner in a special house. I went into the [former] room; Mr. Weiser was there. The evening meal was prepared and we were invited to the table. Thereupon the following made their appearance: Mr. Lewiston,[107] his wife, 2 sons, 1 daughter, the inspector, the secretary, Madem[oiselle] and the both of us. The gentleman said that he had 5 additional children, 3 sons and 2 daughters, who did not come to dinner, however.[108] After dinner was ended, we spoke about several indifferent matters until we felt like retiring. We were lighted into a room, which with respect to elegance was not in want of anything—at least in my opinion. Everywhere, there were portraits of the grandfather Lewiston; large mirrors of different sizes increased the elegance. In the bed, to which we were assigned, we arranged ourselves as comfortably as ever in the somber Spanish style. The next day, the 25th of the month, we decided to take the road across on the <u>ferry</u> and then to Schoharie.[109] Mr. Lewiston advised us to do so since the roads [that we had intended to take] were not well constructed and we would do better to go via Albany; Mr. Weiser agreed to that and we started early. They wanted to keep us for breakfast but since

---

[103]Weiser (Wallace 1945: 10) writes: "Here in levingston or as the High Germans say Lewenstein's Manor."

[104]The Upper Manor House, built about 1690, was on the east bank of the Hudson several miles north of East Camp, near the mouth of the Roeliff Jansen Kill (DHNY 3: map at 414; Dangerfield 1980: 13–14).

[105]At the mouth of the Roeliff Jansen Kill, where there were facilities for the manor's sailing vessels (Bruce E. Naramore, pers. comm., August 1992).

[106]Claus writes "frigatine."

[107]Livingston.

[108]At the time of Claus's visit, Robert Livingston, Jr. and his wife, Maria Thong, had eight children: Philip, Peter Robert, Maria, Walter, Robert Cambridge, Catherine, Alida, and John (Dangerfield 1960).

[109]Claus spells this "Jochery."

we had to cover 40 miles to Albany, we rendered thanks for the
many courtesies. We set out and after 20 miles, we arrived at the
little market town of Kinderhook where after eating the midday
meal we immediately continued on our way. When it became
dark, we went into an inn on this side of the river toward Albany,
where we were well taken care of overnight. Sunday morning,
the 26th of August, we were rowed across the water and took our
lodging in Albany with an acquaintance of Mr. Weiser by the
name of Albert Rosenbumb.[110] Upon our entering the city on
horseback one of the nobler Mohawks caught sight of Mr. Weiser,
ran over to him and welcomed him. We, however, went on our
way but since it was time to go to church and Mr. Rosenbumb was
really sent to go there, we accompanied him and heard a good
sermon from [the] Dni. The bad singing of the Hollanders, however, rendered the whole service quite disagreeable. We went
home and after having partaken of the midday meal, Mr. Weiser
visited good friends until it was time for the afternoon church
service. I followed his example but after returning home and
spending a few hours with our landlord, an Indian came to us in
a great hurry and waved me to go with him. Following him he
eventually took me to a place where Mr. Weiser was with 2 major
officials of the city and 10 or 12 Mohawk Indians. Among them
were some of the chiefs with whom Mr. Weiser had intended to
negotiate and come to an agreement about the most necessary
items.[111] As the evening approached, the Indians said adieu but
we and the 2 Albanians took our evening meal in the same house
and spent the time with all sorts of discussions. At this time, the
2 mentioned with praise how well the Province of New York was
presently represented by a man who, showing great interest in
Indian affairs, said that he was for stopping the varied attempts
of bringing the French Indians onto this side through a great
many seductions and flatteries. Since he knew how to react to the
Indians' sense of humor, they obeyed him in every way. In the
meantime, it was only regrettable that his many efforts [in deal-
ing] with the daily disturbances on the part of the Indians, who
lived outside the province, were not rewarded. This man was
Cornet Johnson, an Irishman by birth, who had proven himself
useful in the English military service. They [the 2 Albanians] persuaded Mr. Weiser to ride—although somewhat out of the way—

[110]Ahasuerus (Ahasverus) Roseboom (1700–1774?), an Albany merchant (CASHP, case
number 1533).
[111]Weiser (MPC: 470) reports that two of these Indians were the Mohawk chiefs Nickas
and Henry Peters (Hendrick).

in the direction where Cornet Johnson happened to be staying. We got up and these men, Mr. Lydius[112] and Mr. von der Heyden,[113] accompanied us to our lodging. Mr. Lydius, however, asked Mr. Weiser to stop by his house upon his departure and take a letter along to the aforementioned Cornet Johnson. At this point we wished each other good night and left.

Monday morning, while Mr. Weiser had still to take care of something, our host wanted me to have some pleasure and invited me to pigeon-shooting because these ANIMALIA flew over the houses; he had ordered a blind made to clear [his property of them]. After taking the midday meal, we set out and having covered 10 miles until evening, we arrived at a place where a Low-German [by the name of] N. Bancker lived.[114] Over the evening meal he told us about the cruelties that during the last war were committed against the Christians and Indians in this region and against a town, [called] Schenectady, by the French Indians under the command of a French officer, who either murdered them in horrible fashion or led them as prisoners away to Canada; neither he [Bancker] nor his family had been safe at any time from the sudden attacks of this enemy.[115]

On Tuesday, the 28th of th[is] m[onth], we set out early on the way to Schoharie in good weather but because of a badly constructed road we could not progress very fast. On the way, we were riding through a valley when Mr. Weiser told how he together with his father-in-law and several others had once been in Albania [Albany] during wintertime. On their way back, they were overtaken by nightfall and not being able to reach Schoharie, they had to spend the night in the bush with an Indian where

---

[112]John Henry Lydius (1693–1791), trader, interpreter, and land speculator, the son of Rev. John Lydius, was living in Albany in 1750 (SWJP 1: 645 n; cf. Jennings et al. 1985a: 245; cf. Wallace 1945: 249ff.).

[113]Jacob van der Heyden, a freeholder and inhabitant of Albany, was an officer in the Albany Battalion (SWJP 1: 809–10, 7: 455).

[114]This may be John Bancker (b. 1710), whose home was on the road from Albany to Schoharie, directly south of Schenectady (CASHP, case number 6740). Weiser and Claus were traveling in this direction.

[115]In writing Schenectady ["Shenechderdy"], Claus may have misidentified, or was confused about, this event and the town in which it took place. It is true that several men lost their lives or were captured in a skirmish with a party of French and Indians at Malewyck (Scotia), west of Schenectady, in July 1748 (NYCD 6: 443, 446; SWJP 1: 173–74). However, the settlement of Saratoga, today Schuylerville, was attacked by a large force of some 400 French troops and 220 of their Indian allies, under the command of M. Marin, in mid-November 1745. A fort, many houses, several saw mills, and stores of supplies and provisions were burned over a large area populated by whites. Some 100 people were either killed or captured, causing panic in Albany and along the frontier, an episode more in accord with that described by Claus (NYCD 6: 288; SWJP 1: 42–43; cf. Clarke 1940: 125). Wallace (1945: 232–34) says that Weiser became depressed upon hearing the news of this raid.

they were completely snowed in. After 17 miles, we arrived about one o'clock in the afternoon in Schoharie, where Mr. Weiser 20 years and then some ago had lived and thus still had some friend or good acquaintance here and there.[116] We turned in at a Justice [by the name of] Johannes Lawyer,[117] who after lunch led us to a church newly under construction. There we met Mr. Sommers,[118] the minister of the place, who had been sent here from Hamburg [Germany]. This afternoon we walked around the place to visit some acquaintances. The next day Mr. Weiser rode to his half-sister, who lived 10 or 12 miles from Schoharie; I, however, decided to remain in order to get more information about this place and the region as a whole; AB DESCRIPTIO[NE]:[119] Since Mr. Weiser stayed away for 2 days and did not return before the evening of the 30th, we intended to advance a good stretch on the next day. But we could not depart on Friday the 31st before Brack-fest time because the Reverend Sommers accompanied us part of the way under overcast sky. We begged him, however, to stay back at the last plantation while we continued our journey toward the aforementioned Cornet Johnson's place in Mohawk land on a narrow and rather bad Indian path. On the way, however, we were surprised by such a heavy rain that we were completely drenched. [*several illegible words*] place where there was a natural salt-lick and [we] saw that there were various paths made by the animals. Because of this we missed the right way and again got on another unknown to us. As we were now erring along through bush and hedges completely drenched—Mr. Weiser had also lost one flap of his coat as well as the heel of one of his boots—, we finally encountered 2 Indians, one of whom was sick. Mr. Weiser inquired from them whether this path led to Cornet Johnson's but they did not want to understand any of this but said that this was a way to Schoharie and that we were 5 miles off the beaten path and if we had stayed on the right way, we could by now be at the desired place. Fate had been both favorable and unfavorable to us for if we had not encountered the Indians, we could have reached no place anymore in daylight and would have had to spend the night in the bush in drenched clothes without having eaten or drunk. Quite willingly, we

---

[116]Weiser had lived in the Schoharie Valley from about 1712 until 1729 (Wallace 1945).

[117]Johannes Lawyer was a resident of Schoharie. In 1723, he, together with Weiser and Peter Wagoner, purchased a parcel of land on Otsquago Creek in the Mohawk Valley (SWJP 5: 265–77; Wallace 1945: 34, 162).

[118]Peter Nicholas Sommers (Somer, Sommer, Somner) became the Lutheran minister at Schoharie (Brunnendorf) in 1743 (Muhlenberg 1942, 1: 249; ERNY 5: 3400).

[119]'According to the layout'.

turned around with our guides and after crossing the Mohawk River reached the English Fort Hunter[120] at nightfall. This castle[121] had a garrison of *[left blank]* soldiers,[122] otherwise most of the inhabitants were Indians [who lived] in houses built of treebark. We had to take up quarters at one of the Indian chiefs, by the name of Brant, in German, Brand, and we really could not find fault with it; for he lived in a well built, 2 story house, provided with furniture like that of a middle-class family; there was nothing wanting in our food or drink or in our beds. In the morning, we had a good breakfast. We then wanted to pay our respects to the commanding officer, Capt. Butler,[123] but he must already have heard of Mr. Weiser's arrival wherefore he anticipated us in making the [special] effort to come to our lodging.

After informing himself now about this piece of news now [*sic*] about that one from Mr. Weiser, he [turned to me] asking from which country I was and how I happened to be on this journey. Complying with his wish I answered him whereupon he told how he had gotten around quite a bit in northern Germany, yet no farther than the Rhine River while he was in [the] English Military Service. He wanted to take us to his lodging but since we had to hurry on, we asked him to excuse us and hastened to get to Johnson's, which we accomplished after covering 3 additional English miles. At 9 o'clock in the morning we stopped by the aforementioned plantation of Cornet Johnson and asked whether he was at home.[124] He came out immediately and invited us into his room. Mr. Weiser delivered his letter whereupon he asked where we came from and how far we intended to go. Mr. Weiser gave him the answer. He [Johnson] said that last Thursday a gentleman (mailing address: Kalm staying in Philad. at present), sent by the Royal Swedish Academy of Science, had departed for Albany from here after having stayed a few days

---

[120]Located at the mouth of Schoharie Creek, this was the "lower" Mohawk Indian village, established about 1710.

[121]"Castle" was used frequently in the seventeenth and eighteenth centuries to refer to a fortified Indian village.

[122]In 1754, twenty-five soldiers were stationed at Fort Hunter (NYCD 6: 924).

[123]John Butler (baptized 1728, died 1796) was a British agent and interpreter among the Indians (Jennings et al. 1985a: 232).

[124]Johnson built his second home in the Mohawk Valley, "Mount Johnson," about 1739. This was a one and one-half story stone house east of Kayaderosseras Creek. Within a few years he began construction of a third home just west of the creek, which would be called Fort Johnson, moving into the unfinished structure in January 1750. Claus (1904: 5) described it as "a large Stone House with two Wings." In 1762, Claus married Johnson's daughter Ann (Nancy), and the couple were invited to live at Mount Johnson. It was burned during the Revolutionary War (SWJP 1: xvii–xviii; Hamilton 1976; 37–38; Pound 1930: 86; Smith 1906: 91).

with him.[125] He had come from Onondaga and on his trip had
made various observations about plants and herbs. He [Kalm]
had also told him about all sorts of things which he had re-
searched as something very special with the Indians; among others he had asked him [Johnson] about the geometrical shapes of
flowers and how the Indians executed their salicalion cures[126]
with little effort and without any danger to their life. He [Kalm]
had been most interested in it and asked Mr. Johnson to do him
the great favor of sending out a few Indians after the seeds before
he returned. He [Johnson] promised him to do so. It turned out
a bit different because even for the Indians they [the seeds] were
something very rare to get a hold of. But yesterday the Indians
arrived with the seeds; so today he sent out 2 young Indians to
bring him live rattlesnakes, which Mr. Kalm had also requested.
All this would please Mr. Kalm when he returned. Mr. Weiser
gave him [Johnson] to understand that he regretted not to be able
to meet said gentleman here as they had agreed in Philadelphia
to meet each other in Onondaga. Mr. Johnson replied that he expected him tonight according to [the message that] he [Kalm] had
left behind whereupon Mr. Weiser decided to remain. In the
meantime, various Indians, acquaintances of Mr. Weiser, came
by, greeted him and sat down with him. Mr. Johnson mentioned
that since the last war,[127] the Indians all of a sudden no longer
came to his house and only sporadically did one or the other drop
in without, however, wanting anything. One should not be an-
noyed that it made no great difference to them whether these
were times of war or peace since anyway every means was em-
ployed by France to win the English Indians over to their side.
And indeed, a French clergyman[128] was placed at the border, who
was provided with all the materials belonging to the Indian at-
tire. When one or the other English Indian or their children came
to him, he welcomed them very amicably, took them into his
store and whatever clothes they chose, he would order them
made completely gratis for them; such things made a great impression on these people. It was the same with the religion, and
since the French knew that the Indians were great admirers of

---

[125]Peter (Pehr) Kalm (1716–1779), the eminent Swedish botanist and natural historian,
and a student of Linnaeus, had arrived in Philadelphia in 1748 (Kalm 1966).

[126]The phrase "salicalion cures" is probably a reference to medicines derived from the
Salicales, an order of plants coextensive with the family *Salicaceae*. (*Salix* 'willow tree', has
aspirin-like qualities.)

[127]King George's War (1744–1748).

[128]A reference to Abbé François Picquet, a Sulpician missionary at La Présentation (Os-
wegatchie), a French fort and mission near what is now Ogdensburg, New York (Claus
1904: 5; Blau et al. 1978: 494–95).

[French] pictures and decorations catching their [the Indians'] eyes with their extremely beautiful French adornments, they presented their religion to these people through all those pictures. Besides, he [Johnson] wanted to do all kinds of things as, e.g., giving the Indians provisions of ammunition from his own bag together with 4 pockets full of advanced money, which [originally] was to be paid to the province. He then led us into a room where he kept his library in a safe place together with his globe and other rarities as, e.g., Indian weapons of war. Among them were 1 spear, 2 big arrows and 1 club whose head was of black agate. It was completely round with a little hollow out of which they also smoked; it was about one hand long and the haft about 2 Schl.[ag] long.[129] When they defended themselves with it, the blow landed either on the chest or in between the shoulders.[130] Otherwise, Mr. Johnson was rather well provided with a blunderbuss, rifles, muskets and other guns. He also had a charming scarlet and silver habit, which he wore in the last war since he himself had to face great danger and much worry although his house was surrounded by block houses. He likewise led us around the house, whose upper part was still under construction. But as could be judged from the lower part and other features, nothing would be wanting in it in regard to comfort and elegance once it was finished. Anyway, Mr. Johnson showed us many courtesies and treated us well as we drank a good glass of wine first of all to the head of the country and to his own superior but then, we did not forget those we left at home in Germany.[131]

The bigger of Mr. Johnson's dogs makes everyone laugh. When I sat down near him, he came at once, looked at my shirt buttons, ring, boots and spurs and as I, coming from the bush, still had some [leaves or twigs] hanging down from the bottom of my coat, he neatly took them down from me. But when his master came along and had something to eat for him, he embraced, kissed and pressed him to his heart. When he offered him watermelon[132] and bread, he took each in one of his paws and ate them in turn like a human. Mr. Johns[on] said that this animal was a great lover of dram. When the hogshead in the cellar had been opened,

---

[129]"Schlag," an old German measure equal to about one foot.

[130]In his journey to Onondaga in 1743, John Bartram (1973: 49) noted that while at Tioga on the Susquehanna River, the Indians "sat down and smoaked their pipes, one of which was six foot long, the head of stone, the stem a reed." However, the combination pipe and club described here is characteristic of Indian cultures of the eastern Plains. Johnson was an avid collector of Indian material culture and had acquired a number of objects from groups in the west (Burch 1990).

[131]The papers of Sir William Johnson are silent regarding the Weiser and Claus visit.

[132]Claus writes, "Wasser Melons."

he [the dog] smacked around the tap and rattled it until it poured out and all ran onto the floor. This caused great damage not only to him, but also to the many pelts of wild animals that were stored there; the young moor had to be baptized by force.

On Sunday morning, Sept. 2, we departed in hot weather which, however, turned cooler after a rain shower. We walked along the Mohawk [River] on a rather good road and passed through one of the most fertile regions of which I had learned before and now saw for myself. It was only regrettable that the people who cultivated it were so poor that they left the best land untilled and only hoed around the edges; bears and wolves also did much damage. After covering 25 miles we came to one Barthol Pickert, the brother of Mr. Weiser's brother-in-law. On Monday, the 3rd of th[is] m[onth], several good acquaintances accompanied us to Mr. Weiser's sister. Since on the way we visited a man, called Nie Fuchs,[133] who was more than 100 years old, we did not arrive at the sister's house before 2 o'clock in the afternoon. Because M. W.'s horse while being shod had been injured by the Smith John, he had to rent another from that one's brother-in-law; at the same time they took one of his sons, N[ie][134] John, along, who took care of the provisions that were prepared for the bush.

Thus we departed on Tuesday, the 4th and traveled up to Jost Hercheimer in Burnets Field where we spent the night. Because a Tapper[135] had provided us with traveling expenses, we also ordered the horses shod.

On Wednesday morning, the 5th, we hurried off and came to a settlement not far from there, called *[left blank]*, and 12 miles farther to the last plantation inhabited by white people, which a certain Nie Jerg Cost inhabited.[136] Since we were unable to reach any Indian settlement that same afternoon, we did not want to continue our way that night. He [Cost] entertained us well and was happy that we had visited with him because he had come

---

[133]In 1713, John Christian Fuchs, Johann Conrad Weiser (Weiser's father), and several other Palatine Germans, went to the Mohawks seeking permission to settle in the Schoharie Valley (NYCD 5: 575). "Nie" may be an abbreviated form of "Dominie," used here as an honorific in addressing the elderly Fuchs.

[134]"Nie" here might suggest "Master John."

[135]Tavern-keeper.

[136]Claus (1904: 5) writes that upon leaving Fort Johnson, the party "proceded to Stonearabia [Stone Arabia, a Palatine settlement], Canajee. [Canajoharie] _____ * [illegible in the original manuscript] Flatts." The "illegible" word in Claus' *Narrative*, and the word left out here in his journal, is "German"; that is, German Flats, the vicinity of Herkimer, New York.

over the ocean with Mr. Weiser. He also mentioned with satisfaction what a good livelihood he had made for himself at this place. The Indians visited him quite often and never departed empty-handed. It was only quite unpleasant when they came drunk because they were then apt to take whatever they could find; if one hindered them, the evil only grew worse. Of late he had the experience that an Indian had taken his [Cost's] food from the fire and when he pushed him away, he [the Indian] went out and returning with his gun shot dead 2 young, strong horses. On Thursday the 6th, we prepared for the trip, provided ourselves with mats[137] because the Savages [Indians] had no beds or such things. I took a new horse since the former was sore from the long journey and there was anyway not much opportunity to find fodder among the Indians. We then set out into the wilderness accompanied by a man, who was headed for Oswego to free his brother from a band of French Indians, who had come during the last war, plundered one of the outlying houses and shot the eldest son dead in it with a gun and 2 arrows. They took the younger as hostage to Canada together with a dependent brother, who had run out in the path. Since he had heard that the pastors there let these [hostages] come to them at will, he wanted to do his utmost and send an Indian of his acquaintance, who should discuss the matter with those Indians there to give orders to free these children. This man's road, however, separated from ours and we took leave from one another. Riding on a very bad road where the horses were often stuck in mud up to their bodies and the sky in addition afflicted us with something from above, after 11 hours we arrived at the Indian Castle Oneida, which was lying on a height.[138] [*The following sentence is written in the left margin*]: Meeting a stranger, the curiosity of the Indians does not go further than [to know] where he came from, whether his business was of their concern and whether he would continue on his way. Everybody came out as we were climbing up. According to their custom, a deputy was sent out, who had to get information about where we came from and what we desired. Having been given the appropriate answer, he retreated again and then showed us our place of residence, which was one of the more dis-

---

[137]Claus uses the German word *teppich* 'rug'.

[138]This is probably the Oneida village of Anajot (Beauchamp 1916: 133ff.) or "Old Oneida" (Kirkland 1980: 132–33, 144, 159, 350), visited by the Moravians David Zeisberger, J. Martin Mack, and Gottfried Rundt in 1752. It was located near present-day Vernon Center.

tinguished [houses] because a gray pole with intermittent red stripes stood in front of it.[139] On the outside, they [the houses] were entirely built of bark [and were] about 12 or 13 Schlag wide [*sic*] and 18 or 20 high [*sic*].[140] Inside, they were divided on both sides into several rooms, which were rather well fit together with posts and boards, on which one could sit or lie; on both sides, boards were also nailed below so that one could put something behind. These rooms, of which there were 3 to 6 on each side of the house, appeared to me like box-beds without doors. In the middle of the corridor, which was 5 or 6 Schlag wide, a fire was burning in front of each [room] for cooking and on top goods and victuals were laid. The seat was about 2 Schlag high from the floor. On top, [smoke] holes of about 40 or 50 and more Schlag long will be kept open, which did not suffice, however, for all the smoke to escape. So we were led there. In front of the door, there lay a young black bear, that upon seeing white people coming made himself appear as wild as if he had never been tamed. Then we were shown our box [room] and after we had arranged ourselves, corn bread was given us, that had been baked in hot corn husks[141] N.B. Ahead of time, the Indian corn was pounded with hard blows in a hollowed stump, about 2 Schlag high, then wetted with water and ashes put into it. Just on this day, the Indians had a feast for they all appeared in regalia. Soon afterwards, their music was heard playing for a dance with an instrument formed like a snare drum but emitting the sound of a kettle drum. There ensued a great shout of joy before the dance began. When I heard that they were about to begin, I approached the house, which was rather long, and wanted to watch from a distance. But without any harm being done to me, I was pushed and pulled in and had to sit near a fire, around which they presently formed a circle and danced in a solemn and upright manner; a woman well advanced in years went in front and a young Indian followed, who repeatedly called out several words which the rest shouted after him. I watched them for about half an hour and since it was already night, I went to our lodgings where we lay down to sleep. The next morning, the 7th, a man came and announced to Mr. Weiser that the council had assembled to hear what his diplo-

---

[139]A "war post" or "striking post."

[140]Claus meant to say twelve or thirteen Schlag *high* and twenty *wide*, rather than the reverse. In 1743, Bartram (1973: 58–59) described what may have been the same house at Onondaga as about seventeen feet wide and eighty feet long, with a center aisle six feet in width.

[141]Corn bread was sometimes baked by wrapping uncooked loaves or cakes in corn husks and placing them in the hot ashes of a fire.

matic mission to them entailed and what would be asked of them. He [Mr. Weiser] therefore went to the place where they led him. The speaker introduced his commission and immediately thereafter sent a messenger to Onondaga to make our arrival known so that the rest of the Nations could be called together. After the council had ended, we were invited by one of the chiefs for the midday meal, which we could not refuse. We therefore arrived at the appointed time and after sitting down, a hen and corn cake boiled in chicken broth was put in front of each in a big wooden bowl and after this a goodly number of apples, which, however, like everything grown in the woods did not have much taste. At the end, we were treated to flute music played by a young Indian. Having rendered our thanks, we returned to our lodgings and prepared for continuing our journey to Onondaga. Of all the strange oddities that happened here, I cannot mention any other as true than that a horn or an antler was given me by someone when we came to a house that lay a little off the main path. When we entered, we were shown the English flag that had been stuck on the house. It [the antlers] was three spans long, had 1 full breadth, was 2 thumbs thick and had 8 ends [tines]; there we also saw a peculiar kind of snowshoes.

Oneida
    arrival;
    welcome;
    lodging;
    dancing;
    council and summoned to Onondaga;
    the big horn was 6 inches wide; the ends
    18 inches long; with 8 ends [tines].
    at a chief for dinner
    where the elk [antler] was exhibited;
    treated to a corn cake, sour apples
    and flute music;
    young bear flitting about;
    a pair of snowshoes.
    The following day through an Indian place;
    drum beating; an Indian in the woods;
    death of the chief of Onondaga.

On Tuesday, the 28th, we wanted to set out early but were advised that this morning some warriors would depart for South Carolina against the so-called flat heads or Catabaw Indians; we wanted to see this. Half an hour later, however, we were told that they would not go today because the trial by fire had not given a satisfactory answer to the question whether this would be a good time to set out against the enemy. Thus we went away and after one English mile we passed an Indian settlement of Tuscaroras.[142] These Indians beat the drums and stood much decked out in front of their houses; we, however, did not stop but rode through the bush on a hilly and sandy road. We stopped at noon and ate a cold meal under a tree not far from a fresh water on a plain where the horses found their pasture at the same time. We did not rest for long because we were in a bit of a hurry; so we continued. Riding quite a stretch in the bush, we met an Indian hunter with the message that Canasatego, the chief of the 6 Nations, had grown pale in death a few days ago.[143] Mr. W. was alarmed and considered our long journey in vain because in such a case no council would be assembled. But when we arrived in the assigned night's lodging at Canasoragy, which consisted of but several mats, we were received because our arrival had been made known in all Indian settlements through the messenger, who had been sent out by the Oneidas. They immediately led us to the house just repeating [the fact of] the death of their chief. With all that, the Onondagas announced that seeing that Mr. W. had come this far on his journey, he should just continue and against their tradition they would call the council together and listen to him. This declaration delighted Mr. W., the more so because the Indian, who had come to us in the forest, had not mentioned anything about that.

Early on Sunday morning, the 9th, we set out—because the Indians do not differentiate between days—and were accompanied to Onondaga by an old Indian, who was a council member. Mr. W. took his lodging in the [same] inn to which he had been assigned the first time[144] and was welcomed by the landlord with a deep French bow, which he must have learned in Canada. Since

---

[142]Possibly the village of Ganatisgoa or Kanadesko, "a Tuscarora town" (Beauchamp 1916: 114ff.) about three miles west of Anajot (Kirkland 1980: 62, 64, 66, 160). "Here we found almost thirty houses, large and regularly built, with a wide street through the middle of the town" (Beauchamp 1916: 114). It was located near what is today Marble Road in the town of Vernon.

[143]Claus (1904: 5; cf. Wallace 1945: 131 n 19) reports that when he and Weiser arrived at Onondaga, "they found the Indians in great Mourning & Grief on acct. of their Head Sachem Canaghsadigo being dead a few days before by Poison which was suspected to have been conveyed into his Victuals by some french Emissaries that then resided at Onandaga Lake under the Disguise of Traders."

[144]This is the same house that Bartram (1973: 58–59) describes in 1743. The landlord was Tohaswuchdioony (MPC: 475).

the 6 Nations live quite near the French borders, they must always keep their neutrality. One or the other remains on friendly terms with the French but the English are generally considered to be closer to them than the French: because for many years his house has been an inn of the Pennsylvanian Rassgr.[?] During the time of our visit he was quite friendly and trusting, even showing us the French pass of his parents.

Thus, we expected the deputies of said Nations on the following Monday but none arrived. On Tuesday, the divination took place, which will be described later. Still no deputy. We awaited the dep[uties] the next following Monday but again heard nothing from the Nations. On Tuesday, I went on. On Wednesday, Mr. Weiser wrote a letter to Capt. [John] Lindesay, commander of Fort Oswego, and at the same time, he issued a pass to a comp[any] of Indians, who wanted to set out against their enemies, the Catabaws of South Carolina. After this, we rode to the castle which lies across the river because the people for lack of wood had drawn back a little farther. As our lodging stands on the previous place all by itself, Mr. W. began to get a little impatient because of the long delay of the dep[uties].

On Thursday, I wanted to ride to the Cath.[olic ?] [illegible word] which lies off about 5 or 6 miles away, but I learned that the warriors would depart and thus I delayed my trip. I then saw them set out with shooting and most solemn singing.

Thereupon our landlord told us about the intentions of the Moravian Bishop Cammerhoff, who while passing by the Penns[ylvanian's] quarters stopped there a few months ago. They immediately noticed, however, that he made weak excuses and notwithstanding his many presents he did not achieve anything. In preserving this relationship in which the Indians contributed moderately in righteous oratory, 4 dep[uties] from the Oneidas and Tuscaroras entered. This was quite à propos and thus Friday was chosen as the day for the assemblage of the councillors. We should not forget to mention that when we awoke on Friday morning, these dep[uties] greeted us with "good morning," which is something very rare with these people. Several of the Oneidas began to pray quite fervently for one quarter of an hour: I heard at various times the n[ame] J[esus] C[hrist] amen whereupon I asked M. W. for an explanation. He told me that a few years ago many proverbs from the Bible and also English prayers had been translated into an Indian language and then sent to a printing press. Since many Indians did not live far from Christians and also professed themselves to be Anglicans, they must have learned these prayers by heart after they had been read to them.

We then readied ourselves to go to the council and the councillors of the Nations together with M. W. went a short way behind the bushes where the latter presented his commission. At every article, he offered a wampum belt, which with these peoples has the value of money. How this is handled with the more advanced of the Indian Nations shall later be explained in detail.[145] Soon thereafter a speaker was chosen among these councillors, who had to recite the articles mentioned before in the public assembly in the form of an oration. At this time a few more from the community of Zargonna[146] Bernsten [?]. As mentioned before, he presented and handed the respective belt to one of the councillors after each paragraph or article. He had to learn the different points verbatim by heart and when he had nothing further to hand out, he continued to recite until all the articles were read. After this solemn act was ended, the entire assembly broke up and went its separate ways into another house to decide on the answer. On Friday afternoon nothing else was being done than to express condolences to the Nations on the loss of their Chief Canas[atego], which constituted the first article. In my opinion, the other articles were admirably recited by the Indian speaker. He stopped at the end of each article whereupon those present confirmed it with one voice or tone. When he had ended, they lay back on their seats and reflected about their answers. Having quietly conversed with each other for about 1 hour, another one was heard, who, however, offered thanks for nothing else but the condolences and promised an answer to the remaining main points on the next day. They then separated and agreed to assemble the following day. We waited eagerly for it [the answer] while the pleasure of being among the Indians always lasted about 10 or 12 days; in the meantime, they even delayed everything further and if the night had not made an end to it, they would have discussed the matter still further because they were rather deliberate in such matters. Finally in the dead of night, the dep[uties] of On[eida] and Tus[carora] appeared reporting that the council had ended but that the final answer must [wait until it would] first be made public in their country, i.e., On[eida] and Tus[carora]. We accepted that but did not know un-

---

[145]Claus does not furnish this promised explanation.
[146]Zargonna (Sorichona), the chief of "lower" Onondaga (Beauchamp 1916: 119, 129).

der what kind of clamor this would happen and immediately prepared for the return trip, which we began the following day, i.e.,
September 16. We arrived in Canasoragy in overcast weather together with this company of dep[uties] and a chief of Onondaga
on the same day. There, we spent the night in the house of a
rather young Indian since in every place, there were completely
free lodgings for travelers usually with a chief; these people considered it an honor and liked to give whatever they were able to.
At our arrival, they presented us with spansteck [?], a kind of
small pumpkin cooked very little but pleasant to eat as well as
corn, which was prepared in 2 country ways.[147] Our traveling
companions, however, had seen a wild animal on the way, similar to a fox but for the color. They had discovered it in a tree,
which they hewed down; they then beat the animal[148] to death
with clubs. After boiling it for dinner, we all ate it with great appetite. The Indians were very fond of dram and did not refrain
from it until they were drunk and then began to commit life-
threatening actions. These here must have found out that dram
was available in this house. Complaining about many knocks
they had to suffer on the way, they asked M. W. for reimburse-
ment in the form of a bottle, which he let them have. But once
having started, they could not stop and because none of them
had any money, M. W. would let them pay with a sleeping blan-
ket and a knife. Thus the chief of Onondaga took off his shirt and
asked for dram to be brought. As he now sensed that he soon
would no longer be master of himself, he took his knife, which
was hanging around his neck, and handed it to me for safe-
keeping. He gave me to understand that he had held it before on
his bare chest and now rendered it to me so that no misfortune
would arise; in the same way, he asked me to keep his satchel
with his pipe and its appurtenances in order to keep them from
being spent on drinking. There was no stopping until the little
barrel had to be brought back and they were convinced that nothing was in the house anymore. Meanwhile we did take along the
one whom M. W. had tried to prevent from drinking as much as
possible, and who had also been the speaker at the council. He
had also promised to call the councillors in Oneida together and
had led M. W. there although these did not come along. We then
arrived *[Claus ends his description of this episode here, and then writes
a second version, which follows.]* They continued, however, until the

---

[147]Claus may be referring to a Jerusalem artichoke *(Helianthus tuberosus)* which resem-
bles a small pumpkin.
[148]A raccoon.

little barrel, that they had gotten ahold of, was empty and they were convinced that nothing was left anymore; finally the hosts and the guests were all full including the speaker, who was appointed to give the answer. He had been kept back as much as possible, because he was supposed to go with us to Oneida on the following day and to bid us farewell but he had lain down, taken [back] his shirt and was completely drunk. Thereupon, we too lay down to sleep, but the moaning took place mostly in front of our bedroom throughout the night. Since this type does not sleep when drunk, we, as is easy to presume, could not sleep very much either for they frequently had a dispute and insisted on getting in a fight. But since the axe and the knife had been stored away and they did not like to use their fists, they would eventually quiet down again. We ardently longed for the break of day and as soon as it became dawn, the horses were taken from the pasture and we hurried to get away from these people.

That the Indian Nation is burdened with many superstitions can easily be observed from the following examples, which I witnessed myself. It happened on the 2nd day after our arrival in Onondaga that a young Indian woman came into our lodging house, who must have been just a few days away from being brought to childbed. She did not act as was to be expected from her condition, however. Indian women in general pay little attention to it, frequently just going into the woods, giving birth to the child and afterwards taking as little care of themselves as they did before. But this one evidently must have had some extraordinary discomfort for she felt like lying down; according to her attestations, she was in great pains. We were at that time provided with all the particular [medicines] from our country, [purchased] in the pharmacy in Halle [Germany], and as Mr. W. could no longer stand this person's whining, he decided to give her a dose of the ESSENTIA DULCIA[149] with some water and dram. After she had taken it, she felt quite a bit better. But these Superstitieus[150] people were not satisfied and wanted to know what kind of sickness it was, where it came from and how it could be gotten rid of. They therefore sent at night for the man, whom they believed to have the spirit of a soothsayer. They asked him to come the next day and seek counsel from the oracle about these matters. The soothsayer appeared the following day and determined the place where he was to practice his art, which was directly in front of the

---

[149]'Sweet matters', medicine that had a calming effect.
[150]Claus writes this word in large Roman letters, capitalizing the initial "s."

sick-bed. His aides then erected there something with pieces of
bark, which covered half his body; the whole resembled a cage,
big enough for one person. Four staves were tied on top, which
were pulled together at their intersection. The cage was closely
hung with mats, and several well heated stones were brought in.
The man completely naked then sat down on the floor, which
was spread with grass. The mats were well fastened behind him
and as I could surmise from his voice, he made his initial speech.
Then followed a penetrating singing and a road to hell[151] with
conversation accompanied by intermittent singing and sighing so
that the soothsayer through the heat of the stones and the mats
and through trying to roll his eyes got into a supernatural state.
In that condition he took a ribbon, put it around his neck and
what then appeared to him in form of an animal or in another
monstrous shape was the means by which to chase away the
spirit of the illness. If it was an animal, it had to be completely
eaten in one meal; if, however, it was a monster or even the devil,
whom they imagined as something horrible, he had to be urged
to come and drive out the spirit of the illness with deafening
noise. Climbing out of his exorcism cell completely drenched [in
perspiration], he granted, just as he was told, that the medicine
we had given was quite good but some of his herbs had also to be
used, which he prescribed. He would order the foe of the illness'
spirit to come later tonight, however, since everything had to be
cleared and covered beforehand. For his efforts he received a
small portion of victuals and marched off. Night began to fall and
the patient had been taken back into the house. Then, we heard
a loud noise from afar. When it got closer, 3 horrible figures with
masks and all sorts of traps fell into the door like savages. Also
some agile figures with long staffs [of wood] and large rattles in
their hands stormed in with great uproar and yelling, spreading
around anything they could snatch up in the house so that the
ashes rose up out of the vent holes like a dense smoke.

Together with some others we had distanced ourselves beforehand and the Indian in whose house all this was happening
asked us to give each of the devils a pipe when they came to us.
We prepared them [the pipes] at once and when they came to us,
we handed them over; thereupon they departed with the same
impetuosity as before [when they had entered].[152]

---

[151]Claus writes, *Helstraze,* literally, 'road to hell'.

[152]Claus is describing a kind of shaking tent ceremony similar to the one observed by
Bartram seven years earlier (1973: 50–51). With much more detail, Bartram (1973: 60–61)
also describes one of Claus's "atrocious figures" or "devils," as a "comical fellow" wear-

In rather rainy weather the road to Johnson's from Schoharie in 5 miles during the night; [met] 2 Indians on the road.

Sunday: to Onondaga from Canasoragy
Monday: awaited the dep[uties] in vain
Tuesday: soothsaying
Wednesday: O[153]
Thursday: under the Ritlnag [?] to the castle; the warriors set out; some deputies from Oneida, Tuscarora and Onondaga [arrived];
Friday: council meeting

The End

Various Words and Idioms Used Among the Indians[154]

human being	uaque	meat	owaro
body		cabbage	onúnsy
		ear	
		corn	conisto
		kernels	
head	onúnsy	milk	anunta
hands	ochsnuchsa	apples	gahig
feet	ochsída	tree	garúnda
eyes	onochoyes	fire	och ista
nose		air	jawody
mouth		earth	ochwenschia
chin		forest	garhágo
teeth		mountain	jonundy
beard		big city	canadajengo
ears	ohughda	town	canadájo
schlest [?]		small	caniwa
neck		big	akowána
throat		spoon	addúgua

---

ing a "clumsy vizard of wood colour'd black, with a nose 4 or 5 inches long, a grinning mouth set awry, furnished with long teeth, round the eyes circles of bright brass, surrounded by a larger circle of white paint; from his forehead hung long tresses of buffaloes' hair, and from the catch part of his head ropes made of the plated husks of *Indian* corn . . . He carried in one hand a large staff, in the other a calabash with small stones in it for a rattle, and this he rubbed up and down his staff."

[153]"O," i.e., "nothing."

[154]Claus compiled what is essentially a German-Mohawk word list (Claus 1904: 6). Eighty-eight of the ninety-four entries are recognizably Mohawk. Of the six remaining, one is Oneida, *waterum* 'nine'. Two others, although they may be Mohawk, do not correspond to any modern forms. These are *jaworec* 'death', and *ochschwenschia* 'earth'. Two entries, *jawody* 'air', and *agosa* 'carpet', do not appear to be Mohawk. Gunther Michaelson (pers. comm., March 1992) is of the impression that this list was compiled by an interested but inexperienced person with an untrained ear, which accurately characterizes Claus in 1750. In just a few years, however, he became one of the most competent and influential interpreters in the province.

belly		knife	ahshary
heart	owery	hungry	cadachcáriak
lung		man	etchyn
liver		woman	akonhechdy
spleen		girl	gajádas
intestines	athun	boy	anageghdera
life		child	agojé
to hear	adhundaz	father	raginiha
to taste		mother	istoha
to feel		brother	jodadegó
to smell		sister	" "
to see	gadgáchto	grandfather	raxotá
thigh		grandmother	axotá
knees		horse	akochschadys
calves		cow	dianhusquarondy
fingers		stag	scanónso
toes		pig	quesques
death	jaworhec	dog	erhard
to die		carpet	agósa
to eat	sadacyny	jacket	adiadouwit
to drink	och nagira	shoe	aghdachqua
bread	canádareck	stocking	garisk
water	hachnéga	pants	gakhaty
dram	hudchgárat	shirt	neadaráha
wine	jochjucis	gun	gahóry
salt	zikeda	arrow	gajenquery
	sugar		
butter	otstutzera	bow	
eggs	onhughsa	shoot	
lard	otstutzera	draw the	
		bow	
flour	othésara	tobacco	ganún
		pipe	
house	ganúghsode	one	huska
easy chair	canaáchya	two	dickony
powder	ogáhra	three	achsa
grains of tin	ochstróqua	four	katéry
much	canaáckery	five	wisky
little	ganigóho	six	sajack
bad	iwagsta &	seven	chadak
	canasquaksy	eight	satésy
good	fojennery	nine	waterum
day		ten	ojery
night			
noon			
evening			

Photo: Luc Chartier, (ANQ)

expensive	canorum
beans, peas	sahéta
& the like	
Where do you come from?	gahajaghsachgidy
Where are you going?	gawaghsa
What is the name of?	othenon quajaz
gruel	jorochsadaragaranijeta
yes	tho,
	nee affirmative
no	jachtá

Indian Prayers[155]

The Creed[156] Teggeniskorighware. Tewagightaghkough Niy-
ohsera gough ne Raniha ne Agwegough tihaeshatste raonissouh
ne karonia, neoni oghwhensja; Neoni Jesus Christ, seragoughra,
ough ha ag Rahawak Songgwa, ganer, ne Tihoyeghtagh Roughne
ne Ronigoghriyough stough, ne rodooni yaghte Kanagh Kway-
enderi Maria ne Roronghya geagh finitiaweniyoughne Pontius

---

[155]Claus writes "*Indianische Gebether* or Indian Prayers."
[156]This prayer is written in the Mohawk language.

Photo: Luc Chartier, (ANQ)

Pilatus tehonwayadaen, haro raongh heyyough neoni ron waya-
dat nagough rawonoughtough ne onesseagth, ne assugh, ni-
wighniferagighhadont, nisat, ketskweagh, nesinihawehey-
youshne ne teshodeagh karonghyage; kawe, noughtough yehein-
derough George, neoni eghjeder, ne raodearaet, Sanigoughriy-
oughstough ne tuitkont Ahathoond adde fina, ahsyere, neoni
areghsagge, saghhahhagough, eghsough Vhiya wedowwane ad-
daddawighsenyokas, roughyage dewightna, eghsough Skeanent-
tharonhegge neoni adas katsera, egsough kaeshatseaght, sero,
ne Alsaggoseane agwegough Sinihoenwagh sweaghse neoni ne
onwa sironhesoghnageangeaonda hoyough siniyeheinwe *[left
blank]* Ahutsenonihagge neoni Adaskat sera, ne rorighooni Jesus
Christ Songgwayaner Amen.

*[The following list of traveling expenses is Claus's. Portions underlined are
translated from the German or French. The remainder were written in English.]*

The following traveling expenses were laid out in the places mentioned before:

Aug.		£	S	d
16	Mrs. Hartley	:00	6	6
17	Trible Piece	:00	00	8
	Sassmann	:00	5	6
18	Heimacher	:00	1	6
	Bethlehem	:00	2	6
	Nazareth Sch: fall:	:00	1	6
	Favour	:00	8	9
19	Language Teacher Dietz[157]	:00	00	9
	Tenant Debois	:00	4	00
	dito to the old Debois	:00	4	00
20	Ferry Delaware-Walpack	:00	1	6
	Rosenkranz Jersey	:00	6	00
	Henrich Cortrecht	:00	8	00
21	Capt. Westbrach	:00	8	00
	Basius	:00	2	6
	Emanuel Basalesh where we had breakfast	:00	4	00
	Gerhard de Witt Mombackes	00	3	00
		£ 2	18	8

Aug. the		£	S	d
22	Lawrens pint wine	:00	1	2
23	Cornelius Elmendorph in Sopus 1 day 2 nights	:1	9	6
	Ferry over Hudsons, Rhinebeck	:00	4	6
24	Lewiston, Lord of the Mannor, over night			
	Philipp Schumacher In Camp at noon	:00	4	00
	very good grapes, berries, and apples	:00	00	00
25	Peter Voncklen	:00	00	8
	Antoni Quakenbush Noon at Kinderhook	:00	4	8
26	Salomon[158] on the other side of the river by Albany where we spent the night	:00	10	00

---

[157]*Sprachmeisterin*, written here, is the feminine form of 'language teacher'.
[158]Salomon Goewey (1687–1758), an Albany-area resident (CASHP, case number 5173).

	by ferry			
	Robert Loatry[159] in Albany, as per appendix	:1	2	9
27	Robert Rosebumb[160] in Albany newspaper and tip	:00	9	00
	In a tap house before Albany 19: of W	:00	2	8
		4	9	2
	brought over	2	18	2
		£	S	d
	brought over	6	19	10
27	Bancker ober night	:00	03	10
till				
28	Jochery Johns Lawyer			
29	3 days	1	00	00
30				
Sept.				
1	the Fort	:00	1	
	Brands son	:00	2	
	The smith two for shoes	:00	4	
2	Col. Johnson for the night	:00	5	
	one shl. in pennys			
	for the boy	:00	1	
	for Dram	:00	00	6
3	to feet for the Horse at			
4	Maquash[161] by his brother in law			
1	french Dollar	:00	08	
5	Henry Hercheimer[162]			
	[in the margin]: can for dram one of [illegible word]			
	Burnet's Field over night			
	& for provisions in the Bush	1	18	00
	a couple of pipes	:00	2	9
6	Georg Cast over night			
	1 rug			
	Canaghwadagy[163]	:00	8	00

---

[159]Robert Lottridge (ca. 1720–1758), an innkeeper (CASHP, case number 453).
[160]Robert Roseboom (1696–1764?) was an Albany merchant (CASHP, case number 1952).
[161]Mohawk.
[162]The son of Johann Jost Herkimer (Jones 1985, 1: 389).
[163]This was the western-most Mohawk village, "the upper Castle of the Mohocks" (MPC: 479).

for dram

		brought over		
		£	S	d
		12	1	11

Sept.

Date	Entry	£	S	d
9	Onontago			
	for 21 etoile[164] dram			
	well mixt with Water	:00	14	00
	the present for the lord	:00	4	00
	[indecipherable word]			
19	Jacob Shwindeman			
	for his Horse			
	Onontago by Kast	:00	8	00
20	Henry Herckheimer over night	:00	10	00
21	Henry fry[165] over night	:00		
	Mohoks Country			
22	to Schoharie			
23	at Shochrys to a			
	qrt. of dram and Wine	:00	5	
24	Niclas Mathis[166]	:00	14	
25	from there to Kats Kill			
26	Niclas Smith, freeholder	:00	2	
	fr. Dietrich	:00	00	3
	the guide Valentin	:00	6	00
		£ 15	5	2
	brought over	£ 15	5	2
	Horses			
26	With Eker over night	:00	1	00
	only for oats			
	Hurley Tab. & Dram	:00	2	6
	Law 1 p. of wine	:00	1	2
	Mombackes Dinner	:00	—	9
27	Andreas de Witt ov n[167]	:00	2	10
	Emanuel Basalesh			
	brakfast &	:00	2	
	for dram			

---

[164]French, 'star'.

[165]Henrick Frey (1680–1763), a freeholder at Canajoharie and a patentee at Stone Arabia, was the brother-in-law of the Reverend Sommers at Schoharie (Jones 1985, 1: 246).

[166]Also Matias or Matheus (b. 1701). A freeholder at Schoharie (Jones 1985, 1: 598).

[167]Abbreviation for "over night."

		:00	00	6
28	Matheus Brank ov night	:00	3	10
	the smith	:00	00	3
	Rosenkranz	:00	01	6
29	Samuel Debois over night	:00	03	9
	Jacob Dietz over the Hills	:00	2	2
30	Bethlehem for the Horses	:00	03	00
	Heymacher	:00	0	6
	Conrad Colb:	:00	05	½
		£ 17	S 4	d 2 ½

Mr. Weiser out of the *[illegible word]*		
at Emanuel Basalesh	S	P
2 pieces of eight	00	16
8 dito at Sopus, *the* 23rd	3	4
in the inn on the way to Albany	1	12
over 4 p: of E.[168]		
In Albany with Robert 2 p: of E: and one and a half		
French taler[169]		

[The following "Extraordinary Memorandum" in English was written by Weiser. The one phrase he wrote in German is underlined.]

Extraord. Memor.

Jadatogo the sister of Cahercerowano desires to be remembered to Mme. Peams.

in Nenochgowy wifes house at Canasarogy we lodged Hankoinwayha his brother-in-law's house Torontaways Ronusuly aquiani.

The Catabaws have killed several persons that offered to be mediators between them and the 6 nations / of the Tutolos and Cherikees / and declared that they will fight them whilst one of the Cata[s] was alive and after their death their very Bones shall still fight the 6 nations.[170]

1 Copy of the treaty in lancaster with the Twitchtwees to be sent to England for the use of the Commiss[rs] for Settling the Boundaries between the English & franch in north America.

The Catabaws speak with too great a Contempt and make themselves unworthy of mercy which the 6 nations. Several thought to

---

[168]Four pieces of eight.

[169]A silver coin used in Germany at this time.

[170]This sentence appears in modified form in Weiser's official report (MPC: 473) and in his journal entry of September 7.

shew had the asked for or folowed the Example of the Cherikees. Two Chiefs of onontago their words to wit Tohaghthwunchiony and his Brother in law. I heard that ontachsima / John Cuir[171] or some such name / the french Interpreter that lay in the Sinniker Country during the late war was gone by the Sinniker Country in his way to ohio with merchant goods and five or six frenchmen with him and told the Sinnikers that he had orders from the Governor of Canada to drive away the English traders from ohio with the assistance of the Indians.[172]

MEMORANDUM TO ONONDAGA *[Weiser writing in English]*

The request of the Ohio Indians To the Council at onontago concerning their share in the lands in pensil.[ia] The letter of Governor South Carolina

The oar[173] on Schahantowaaro to remember what before two years ago in Lancaster *[two words crossed out]* has been treated between the Indians etc.

news at onontago *[Weiser writing in English]*

a hundred of the onontagers are paptist [baptized] by the french priest at Swegatsy and brought before the gove[r] at quebec in very fine trest [dressed] the man all in Silver best Jakits [jackets] and fine coat and great promises made them.

Memorandum *[Claus writing in German]*

When elk claws are available, write to Johnson of Canajoharie as had been promised. Ask Lawyer for strings and elk claws.

[Isolated statements by Claus, writing in German]

From early youth on, I showed an unusual incentive for traveling, and as long as I stayed at home . . .

Since I was for ever more eager to travel to England than to remain in the German Empire but for the English language and some acquaintances . . .

[The following appears to be a list of personal items in Claus's possession, some undoubtedly taken along on his journey to Onondaga. Written in German.]:

---

[171]Daniel-Marie Chabert de Joncaire (ca. 1714–1771), French agent and interpreter among the Indians living in the Ohio region (Jennings et al. 1985b: 233).

[172]This sentence appears, with minor changes, as the entry for September 12 in Weiser's official report (MPC: 476).

[173]A possible reference to a carved, paddle-shaped stick used by Indians as a mnemonic device (cf. Fenton 1950).

BOOKS

Pastors' Bibles in fol.[io]
Castellionis in oct.[a]vo
Hand-Bible from Thüringia
Hymn-Book from Dresden
Gerhard's Exercise in Piety
Erdmann's General Newspaper Compendium
French stories
Handbook in French cover
Book packet in parchment
Schlagbook[174]
Télémaque[175]
   Clothes
Good outfit
Average outfit remains here
3 pairs of pants
Evening clothes
4 pairs of stockings
1 pair of leggings
3 p. of shoes
1 p. of boots   the S 3/38 ls
                    73 t Mg: 63 g t 34

2 hats

                    BED
3 neckbands   1 coverlet and sheet; bolster; pillow
                    2 linen-cloth mattresses 4, 15 shill.

8 shirts
8 undershirts took two along
1 hunting knife   2 sheets and linen for coverlet
1 p. of pistols   2 bolsters
3 caps; took one along   1 pillow-case
4 handkerchiefs   3 napkins
1 pair of silver buckles   2 tin plates and 1 platter
1 hat clasp   knife and fork
  3 undershirts
  1 shirt
2 white caps
1 silk   "
2 pair of linen stockings
2   "   " blue cotton stockings

---

[174]A book of measurements.
[175]The epos by François de la Mothe Fénelon (1651–1715), in which the author indirectly criticizes through allusions the government of Louis XIV.

1 ″ ″ silk   ″ [*sic*]   ″
1 blue cotton handkerchief
3 silk   ″ [*sic*]   ″
2 black neck scarves
1 pair of shoes

REFERENCES

Bartram, John 1973
A Journey from Pennsylvania to Onondaga in 1743. Imprint Society Inc. Barre, Massachusetts.

Beauchamp, William M. 1916
Moravian Journals Relating to Central New York, 1745–66. Dehler Press. Syracuse.

Blau, Harold, Jack Campisi, and Elizabeth Tooker 1978
Onondaga. Handbook of North American Indians, Volume 15:491–99, Northeast, Bruce G. Trigger, ed. Smithsonian Institution.

Burch, Wanda 1990
Sir William Johnson's Cabinet of Curiosities. New York History, Vol. 71, No. 3.

CASHP
Colonial Albany Social History Project. Stefan Bielinski, Community Historian. New York State Museum. Albany.

Clarke, T. Wood 1940
The Bloody Mohawk. The Macmillan Company. New York.

Claus, Christian Daniel 1904
Daniel Claus' Narrative of His Relations With Sir William Johnson and Experiences in the Lake George Fight. Society of Colonial Wars in the State of New York. New York.

Dangerfield, George 1960
Chancellor Robert R. Livingston of New York, 1746–1813. Harcourt, Brace and Company. New York.

DHNY 1850
The Documentary History of the State of New York, 4 vols. E. B. O'Callaghan, ed. Weed, Parsons & Co., Public Printers. Albany.

ERNY 1901
Ecclesiastical Records, State of New York, 7 vols. James B. Lyon, State Printer. Albany.

Fenton, William N. 1950
The Roll Call of the Iroquois Chiefs: A Study of a Mnemonic Cane from the Six Nations Reserve. Smithsonian Miscellaneous Collections, Volume 111.

Glatfelter, Charles H. 1980
Pastors and People: German Lutheran and Reformed Churches in the Pennsylvania Field, 1717–1793, Volume 1, "Pastors Congregations." The Pennsylvania German Society. Breinigsville, Pennsylvania.

Goddard, Ives
1978
Delaware. *Handbook of North American Indians,* Volume 15:213–39, Northeast, Bruce G. Trigger, ed. Smithsonian Institution.
1988
David Zeisberger. *Handbook of North America Indians,* Volume 4:698–99, History of Indian-White Relations, Wilcomb E. Washburn, ed. Smithsonian Institution.

Gollin, Gillian Lindt 1967
Moravians in Two Worlds, A Study of Changing Communities. Columbia University Press. New York and London.

Hamilton, Milton W. 1976
Sir William Johnson, Colonial American, 1715–1763. Kennikat Press. Port Washington, New York.

Jones, Henry A., Jr. 1985
The Palatine Families of New York, A Study of the German Immigrants Who Arrived in Colonial New York in 1710, 2 vols. Universal City, California.

Jennings, Francis, William N. Fenton, Mary A. Druke, and David R. Miller (editors)
1985 (a)
The History and Culture of Iroquois Diplomacy, An Interdisciplinary Guide to the Treaties of the Six Nations and Their League. Syracuse University Press. Syracuse.
1985 (b)
Iroquois Indians: A Documentary History of the Diplomacy of the Six Nations and Their League. Research Publications. Woodbridge, Connecticut. Reading, England.

Kalm, Pehr 1966
Peter Kalm's Travels in North America, The English Version of 1770. Adolph B. Benson, ed. Dover Publications. New York.

Kelsay, Isabel Thompson 1984
Joseph Brant, 1743–1807: Man of Two Worlds. Syracuse University Press, Syracuse.

Kirkland, Samuel 1980
The Journals of Samuel Kirkland, 18th-Century Missionary to the Iroquois, Government Agent, Father of Hamilton College. Walter Pilkington, ed. Hamilton College. Clinton, New York.

Kittle, Walter Allen 1937
Early Eighteenth Century Palatine Emigration, A British Government Redemptioner Project to Manufacture Navel Stores. Dorrance & Company. Philadelphia.

Leder, Lawrence H. (editor) 1956
The Livingston Indian Records, 1666–1723. The Pennsylvania Historical Association. Gettysburg.

Merrell, James H.
1987
"Their Very Bones Shall Fight": The Catawba-Iroquois Wars. In *Beyond the Covenant Chair, The Iroquois and Their Neighbors in Indian North America, 1600–1800*: 115–34, Daniel K. Richter and James H. Merrell, eds. Syracuse University Press. Syracuse.
1989
The Indians' New World, Catawbas and Their Neighbors from European Contact through the Era of Removal. Institute of Early American History and Culture, Williamsburg, Virginia. University of North Carolina Press. Chapel Hill and London.
MPC
A Journal of the Proceedings of Conrad Weiser in his Journey to Onondago, with a Message from the Honourable THOMAS LEE, Esquire, President of Virginia, to the Indians There. Reprinted in 1968 in *Minutes of the Provincial Council of Pennsylvania from the Organization to the Termination of the Proprietary Government*, Vol. 5:470–80. AMS Press. New York.
Muhlenberg, Henry Melchior 1942
The Journals of Henry Melchoir Muhlenberg, in Three Volumes, 3 vols. Theodore G. Tappert and John W. Doberstein, trans. The Evangelical Lutheran Ministerium of Pennsylvania and Adjacent States and The Muhlenberg Press. Philadelphia.*
NYCD 1853–1887
Documents Relative to the Colonial History of the State of New York; Procured in Holland, England and France, by John Brodhead, 15 vols. E. B. O'Callaghan, ed. Weed, Parsons and Company, Printers. Albany.
Pound, Arthur 1930
Johnson of the Mohawks, A Biography of Sir William Johnson, Irish Immigrant, Mohawk War Chief, American Soldier, Empire Builder. The Macmillan Company. New York.
Smith, Richard 1906
A Tour of Four Great Rivers, The Hudson, Mohawk, Susquehanna and Delaware in 1769. Scribner's. New York.
SWJP 1921–1965
The Papers of Sir William Johnson, 14 vols. James Sullivan, Alexander Flick, Albert Corey, and Milton Hamilton, eds. University of the State of New York. Albany.
Wallace, Paul A. 1945
Conrad Weiser, 1696–1760, Friend of Colonist and Mohawk. University of Pennsylvania Press. Philadelphia.

*[*Mühlenberg* the spelling used by Henry Melchior, appears in references to him. The spelling without the umlaut follows, and refers to, printed versions of his work.]

INDEX